EUROPEAN SOCIOLOGY

EUROPEAN
SOCIOLOGY

COMMON-SENSE
IN LAW

PAUL VINOGRADOFF

ARNO PRESS

A New York Times Company

New York – 1975

Reprint Edition 1975 by Arno Press Inc.

Reprinted from a copy in
  The University of Illinois Library

EUROPEAN SOCIOLOGY
ISBN for complete set: 0-405-06493-4
See last pages of this volume for titles.

Manufactured in the United States of America

————◆————

Library of Congress Cataloging in Publication Data

Vinogradoff, Sir Paul, 1854-1925.
   Common-sense in law.

   (European sociology)
   Reprint of the 1914 ed. published by Holt, New York,
which was issued as no. 80 of the Home university library
of modern knowledge.
   1. Law. I. Title. II. Series.
Law   340   74-25793
ISBN 0-405-06545-0

HOME UNIVERSITY LIBRARY
OF MODERN KNOWLEDGE

No. 80

Editors:

HERBERT FISHER, M.A., F.B.A.
Prof. GILBERT MURRAY, Litt.D.,
  LL.D., F.B.A.
Prof. J. ARTHUR THOMSON, M.A.
Prof. WILLIAM T. BREWSTER, M.A.

COMMON-SENSE
IN LAW

BY

PAUL VINOGRADOFF

D.C.L., LL.D., D.HIST., DR.JUR., F.B.A.

CORPUS PROFESSOR OF JURISPRUDENCE IN THE
UNIVERSITY OF OXFORD

NEW YORK
HENRY HOLT AND COMPANY

LONDON
THORNTON BUTTERWORTH

CONTENTS

COMMON-SENSE IN LAW

CHAPTER I

SOCIAL RULES

1. WHEN Blackstone began his Oxford lectures on English law (1753), he felt himself under the obligation of justifying a new academic venture. "Advantages and leisure," he said, "are given to gentlemen not for the benefit of themselves only, but also of the public, and yet they cannot, in any scene of life, discharge properly their duty either to the public or to themselves, without some degree of knowledge in the laws."

Things have moved fast since Blackstone's day, and significant changes have certainly occurred in the educational aspects of law. To begin with, the circle of "gentlemen" who ought to give some thought to laws has been greatly widened : it comprises now all educated persons called upon to exercise the privileges and to perform the duties of citizenship. One need not be a barrister or a solicitor, a member of parliament, a justice of the peace, or even an elector, to take an interest in and feel responsibilities towards laws : all those who pay taxes and own property of any kind, who hire and supply labour, who stand on their rights and encounter the rights of others, are directly concerned with laws, whether they realize it or not. Sometimes a knowledge of law may help directly in the matter of claiming and defending what belongs to one; on other occasions it may enlighten a juror or an elector in the exercise of his important functions; in any case, every member of the community takes his share in the formation of public opinion, which is one of the most potent factors in producing and modifying law.

Again, we must try nowadays not only to acquire some knowledge of the legal rules obtaining in England, but also to understand the aims and means of law in general, to obtain some insight into the processes by which it is formed and administered : for it is only in this way that the meaning of enactments can be realized in a rational and comprehensive manner. Nobody would think it possible to obtain a reasonable view of the causes and conditions which govern economic facts without some knowledge of economic theory. And similarly it would be preposterous to reason on juridical subjects without some insight into jurisprudence.

In view of these obvious considerations, I should like to explain as briefly and simply as possible the main principles which underlie legal arrangements. Although the details of legal rules are complicated and technical, the operations of the mind in the domain of law are based on common sense, and may be followed without difficulty by persons of ordinary intelligence and education. Jurisprudence may be likened in this respect to political economy, which also is developed from simple general principles and yet requires a great deal of special knowledge when it comes to particulars.

In order to realize the aims and characteristics of jurisprudence, it may be useful to consider, in the first instance, what place it occupies as a branch of study. Now study is knowledge co-ordinated by reflection, and as such it is peculiar to mankind; for the most fundamental difference between man and animals consists in man's power of reflection. A dog feels pain and pleasure, is moved

to anger and joy, remembers blows and
caresses, may exercise cunning in achieving
its ends, *e.g.* in opening a gate or in pursuing
game. But its notions, desires and acts
spring directly from its emotions or from
their association by memory. With man it
is different. We also are subject to the
direct impulses of our emotional nature, but
by the side of this direct driving apparatus
in our mind we are conscious of an entirely
different mental process. We are always, as
it were, holding up the mirror to our emotions,
ideas and resolves, and as a result of such
self-consciousness we are living through the
events and actions of our existence not only
in their direct sequence, but also as through
a reflected series. In a direct way the chords
of our spirit are touched from the outside
by the various impressions made by the objects we meet on our way, as well as by
the physiological and spiritual happenings
of our own organism. The process of reflection makes it possible for us to rearrange our
stores of impressions and memories, to co-
ordinate them in accordance with conscious
aims and deliberately selected standards. It
is from this reflective element that men draw
their immense superiority over animals, that

speech, religion, art, science, morality, political and legal order arise.

This observation, drawn from the experience of individuals, is no less apparent in the experience of societies, as recorded by history. Even the most primitive of savages, *e.g.* the Veddas of Ceylon, or the Patagonians, manifest a good deal of reflection in their habits when compared with apes or dogs : only by such means can they build up some rude forms of speech, some notions of supernatural guidance, some account of the order of the surrounding world, some customs of mutual intercourse. Yet the connecting links of their reflection hardly reach beyond the immediate needs and promptings of their rudimentary life. With other tribes the accumulation of knowledge, and its rearrangement and co-ordination by reflection, are the results of a long and arduous struggle in the course of barbaric epochs. It is only comparatively late, in a civilized state of society, that reflective speculation masters every branch of knowledge by the help of science and harmonizes the different sciences by comprehensive philosophy. And as a primitive savage infinitely excels animals through rudimentary reflection, civilized man stands high above the savage by the help of scientific and philosophical speculation. Instead of naïvely responding to primary needs, he surveys and summarizes the experience of innumerable lives of toil and wisdom. The barbarian works out the forms of speech in order to communicate with his neighbours; the modern linguist analyzes the structure of language and the laws of its formation; the barbarian worships mysterious agencies in nature; the modern student of religion tries to account for the evolution of myth and sacrifice, for the mutual influence of creed and morals, for the growth of Church organization.

In the same way, in contrast to the simple rules and divisions of positive law which stretch across the history of all nations, there arises a science of law, a jurisprudence which aims at discovering the general principles underlying legal enactments and judicial decisions. It speculates on the processes of thought which take place in the minds of legislators, judges, pleaders and parties. This theory of law enables men to frame and use their laws deliberately and scientifically, instead of producing them more or less at random under the stress of circumstances. The study of jurisprudence is therefore by no means a mere expedient of the schools, contrived in order to introduce beginners to the terms and principal distinctions of their art, though of course jurisprudence does help in this respect while on its way towards the solution of scientific problems. Nor does our study exist chiefly for the purpose of classifying and cataloguing scattered notices as to rules and remedies : the most perfectly systematized chapters and paragraphs of a code would not render a general theory of law superfluous, for the prime consideration is not so much to establish the sequence of laws as to discover their rational interdependence and ultimate significance. For the intricate maze of a common law which, like the Anglo-American, is based on judicial decisions, the help rendered by jurisprudential classification is especially welcome, nay, necessary; but even apart from that, a theory of jurisprudence is needed to strengthen and complete scattered arguments by treating them as parts of a coherent body of legal thought. Observations and rules which may seem casual and arbitrary when memorialized for practice obtain their justification or call forth criticism when examined in the light of a general theory.

2. It is usual for writers on jurisprudence

to begin with a definition of the topic they propose to discuss, namely, law. But such definitions given at the very outset have this inconvenience, that they are, as it were, imposed on the readers, who as yet have only vague ideas on the subject and therefore are bound to accept more or less passively what is told them in a dogmatic manner. Moreover, a definition of law is by no means easy to give: many have been suggested from time to time, and it is only after careful consideration that one is justified in selecting from the number. It seems more advisable to proceed in a different manner—to clear the way for a definition by narrowing gradually the scope of the inquiry, first determining the class to which the subject belongs, and then marking the particulars of the species under discussion.

It is evident that legal arrangements are a variety of social organization, and that therefore jurisprudence is one of the branches of social science. Man is an essentially social being. Social intercourse is to him a dictate of nature, because he cannot satisfy his wants as an isolated individual; if left to himself, he is, as Aristotle has put it, not self-sufficient. By joining a wife he raises a family; by joining his neighbours in the union of the village he provides for the simple requirements of economic co-operation; by joining fellow-citizens he helps to build up a state which protects him against enemies and enables him to achieve intellectual and moral progress. We can go a step further : if social intercourse is a requirement of men's nature, *order* of some kind is a necessary condition of social intercourse. If a man profits at the expense of his neighbour by snatching away his bread, it will be difficult to establish a community of interests or any amicable intercourse between them. It is only when certain rules of conduct intervene to settle the normal behaviour of men in the exchange of commodities, in the relations of the sexes, or in the regulation of services, that social intercourse becomes regular and continuous.

There are thus certain initial requirements set to those who take part in the association : they ought not to hurt each other, to take undue advantage of each other, to act as if their private wills and pleasures were everything and the wills and interests of their neighbours nothing. Even when two persons join socially for the simple purpose of playing a game of tennis or of chess, they must conform to certain rules in their contest if they wish to achieve their immediate end. The skill or force displayed constitutes the substantive or material part of the game; the rules as to moves and scoring constitute the formal frame of this kind of intercourse. As regards married people, or the shareholders of a joint stock company, or the citizens of a state, the relations involved are much more complex and enduring, but they are substantially of the same kind.

It is evident that laws take their place among the *rules of conduct* which ensure social order and intercourse. Therefore jurisprudence appears among social sciences within the section of so-called *moral* science.

3. Human thought may take up one of two possible attitudes in regard to facts observed by it : it may either watch their relations from the outside and try to connect them with each other as causes and effects, or else it may consider them in relation to man's conscious action, and estimate the connection between ends and means. The first point of view is that of natural science. The second point of view is peculiar to moral science. Let us develop this distinction somewhat more fully.

As soon as we turn our attention to moral science, we perceive two fundamental notions which form the peculiar character of this sphere of study and place it in distinct opposition to our conceptions of surrounding external nature, namely, the notions of will and of reasonable aim. Every one of us is conscious that his acts are produced by his will, in the sense that he has to make up his mind to choose one of many possible courses of action; and this internal experience is opposed to the other way of looking at events as governed by the binding necessity of natural laws. If a connection is established between positive and negative electric elements, a current will be produced, and this event will appear as the application of a law of cause infallibly working under certain given conditions. But when an engineer sets about to arrange an electric battery, every one of his acts in the process is the result of conscious volition, and may be directed to a different end or withheld altogether at any particular moment : the will of the engineer is, of course, influenced by certain causes in a definite direction, but every single act of this will presents itself as the expression of conscious choice.

B

Though the electric current is caused by a certain combination of chemical elements, it is brought about as an end by a series of conscious volitions in the engineer's mind. The consciousness of a moral man is further characterized by its being reasonable, that is, by its submission to judgment according to logical and moral standards. The application of the logical standard does not admit of any doubt or dispute. Whatever may be my likings and wishes, I have to conform to certain logical rules in judging of facts. No amount of selfish appetite will change four apples into forty for me, or alter the rule that two and two make four. But reasonable consciousness goes deeper. No amount of selfish desire can conceal from my reason that what is objectionable to me is objectionable to my neighbour, that it is as bad to kill or rob as to be killed or robbed. There is a story that a savage, on being asked what was the difference between right and wrong, answered : " It is right when I take my neighbour's wife, but it is wrong when he takes mine." I cannot help suspecting that this statement of fact is incorrect and unfair to the intelligence of the savage. No doubt rules which we hold sacred when we ourselves are concerned are often infringed by us : but those who violate such rules become conscious of an antagonism between their reason, which condemns the act, and their passions, which prompted it. A case of conscience arises, and this contradiction between what happens and what ought to happen is at the bottom of all human morality. " The *ought* expresses a kind of necessity, a kind of connection of actions with their grounds or reasons, such as is to be found nowhere else in the whole natural world. For of the natural world our understanding can know nothing except what is, what has been, or what will be. We cannot say that anything in it ought to be other than it actually was, is, or will be. In fact, so long as we are considering the course of nature, the *ought* has no meaning whatever. We can as little inquire what ought to happen in nature as we can inquire what properties a circle ought to have " (Kant).

4. The object of laws is primarily to supply rules of conduct, rules as to what ought to be done and what ought to be abstained from. Laws are, of course, not the only rules of conduct which govern men's actions. People conform also to fashions, to manners and customs, to conventional standards, to pre-

cepts of morality. A man nowadays would hardly care to wear a powdered wig and a three-cornered hat, though he is not positively forbidden to do so. A lady usually puts on mourning after the death of her husband : she considers the black attire and the veil to be prescribed to her by public opinion : and if she chose to disregard the sentiments of others, unpleasant consequences would follow—reprobation, hostile comments, and perhaps the snapping of social ties with friends and relations. As for social custom, it may not be absolutely necessary to greet your acquaintances when you meet them in the street, or to call on them occasionally, but it is customary to do so, and a person careless or casual in such matters is sure to meet with some retribution. Conventional standards are chiefly set up in connection with the habits and manners of certain classes and professions; they are narrower than the common code of morality, but they are intended to be followed by the members of the particular groups concerned. Lawyers and medical men recognize special obligations in regard to professional secrets and professional conduct; mediæval chivalry imposed on members of the *noblesse* very stringent rules of courtesy; and even in our democratic age the code of gentlemanly behaviour and honour demands a considerably greater refinement than the ordinary rules of honesty. Honesty itself, as well as truthfulness, kindness, pity, etc., are moral obligations enforced partly by public opinion and partly by conscience. They are clear expressions of the notion of duty, the precept of the " ought," and a person known to be a liar or a ruffian is certain to excite feelings of repulsion and hostility among his fellow-men.

The rules just described present a kind of scale in which each of the steps supposes stricter obligations than that preceding it. Customary usage is more pressing than fashion; a conventional standard is more imperative than customary usage; and rules of morality are more absolute than rules suggested by a conventional standard. Lastly, legal duties may be said to be more obligatory than moral duties. We notice also various combinations of personal conscience, instinctive obedience and outside pressure. In fashion, the element of personal taste is still very prominent and the sanction of outside pressure relatively slight, evidently because the aim to be attained by following its dictates

is not of great importance. People want to
look like everybody else, or like the better
sort, or a trifle finer still; but even if they do
not succeed the failure is not very damaging :
in such cases, people wear, as it were, a self-
imposed uniform, and the characteristic trait
exhibited is the kind of mimicry which induces
men to select the colours and the cut of their
clothes not in an individual, but in a gregari-
ous way. Customary usage goes further : it is
not a question of looks, but of behaviour, an
expression of supposed feelings, of respect,
friendliness, affection, protection and the like.
There is an aim in all these practices : they
are intended to make the wheels of social
intercourse run easily, to smoothe the relations of acquaintances, friends, superiors and
inferiors by benevolence and mutual consideration; they have to be acquired by
teaching and habit, but ultimately they become almost instinctive. In the case of
conventional standards the aims set by a
community are very conspicuous : the chief
object is to fence off a particular group
from outsiders, and to impress certain duties
on its members. Conventional notions of
this kind may grow to be a kind of secret
doctrine, *e.g.* in freemasonry. Outside pres-

sure increases correspondingly. A person disregarding the rules of the group will eventually be expelled from it. As to moral duties, their social importance is manifest; clearly if the whole or the majority of a given society should be made up of liars and robbers there would be small chance for credit, security and well-being. On the other hand, however coarse a man's moral nature may be, he generally recognizes moral rules in so far as they are likely to guarantee his own interests; and it is very difficult to suppose that one who is in the habit of protecting his own property against thieves would himself turn to stealing without an uneasy sense of contradiction in his conscience.

5. The close relationship between moral and legal notions is striking. No wonder ancient thinkers, Aristotle for example, included the discussion of the elements of law in their treatment of ethics; and for Socrates and Plato the analysis of right was inseparable from the idea of justice. Nor is it a mere chance that in all European languages, except the English, the terms for law and right coincide—*jus*, *Recht*, *droit*, *diritto*, *derecho*, *pravo*—all mean legal order, general rule of law, notion of right on one side, and the

concrete right asserted by an individual on the other. In English, *law* is distinguished from *right*, but rights are based on law, while on the other hand the opposition of right to wrong accentuates the ethical aspect of the notion. Right is that which we find correct, adequate to a certain standard set up by our judgment; wrong is that which is opposed to it. The proposition that two and two make five is wrong according to an arithmetical standard; to repay a benefactor by ingratitude is wrong according to a moral standard; to refuse wages to a labourer may be wrong according to a legal standard, and is certainly wrong from a moral point of view, that is, in the judgment of unprejudiced men and of one's own conscience.

Thus it is certain that law cannot be divorced from morality in so far as it clearly contains, as one of its elements, the notion of right to which the moral quality of justice corresponds. This principle was recognized by the great Roman jurist, Ulpian, in his famous definition of justice : " To live honourably, not to harm your neighbour, to give every one his due." [1] All three rules are,

[1] *Honeste vivere, alterum non lœdere, suum cuique tribuere.*

of course, moral precepts, but they can all
be made to apply to law in one way or another. The first, for instance, which seems
pre-eminently ethical, inasmuch as it lays
down rules for individual conduct, implies
some legal connotation. A man has to shape
his life in an honourable and dignified manner
—one might add, as a truthful and law-abiding
citizen. The juridical counterparts of ethical
rules are still more noticeable in the last two
rules of the definition. The command not to
harm one's fellow-men may be taken to be
a general maxim for the law of crime and
tort, while the command to give every one
his due may be considered as the basis of
private law. And this last precept is certainly not concerned with morals alone : the
individual is not required merely to confer
a benefit upon his neighbour, but to render
to him that which belongs to him as a matter
of right.

The real difficulty arises when we try to
draw a definite line of divison between moral
and legal rules, between ethical and juridical
standards. There are those who would co-
ordinate the two notions on the pattern of
the relation between end and means. They
look upon ethical rules as determining social

ideals, the principles of goodness, virtue, honour, generosity, for which men ought to strive in their personal conduct, and the aims of development, civilization, progress, perfection, which society at large ought to set before itself. Law and laws according to this theory would be the conditions devised for the attainment of such ideals. But such a definition becomes so wide that it includes potentially every case where social influence can be exerted, and one loses the thread of distinction between moral and legal rules. Other jurists have therefore based a distinction on the contrast between theory and practice, or rather between the practicable and the impracticable. In their views law is morality so far as morality can be enforced by definite social action; in other words, it is the minimum of morality formulated and adopted by a given society.

This again is not satisfactory. Many legal rules have nothing to do with moral precepts. If, as the result of the law of inheritance, the eldest son should have his father's estate and the younger brother be cut off with a scanty equipment; or if a statute makes the sale of tobacco a state monopoly : such laws are certainly not suggested by ethical motives.

Besides, even when legal rules are connected directly or indirectly with an appeal to right, it does not follow that they are necessarily framed in consequence of moral impulses. The laws as to bills of exchange or payment of rent are dictated by commercial practice or by established vested interests rather than by moral considerations. In short, numberless aims foreign to the ethical standard play a part in legislation and in legal evolution: national interests, class influences, considerations of political efficiency, and so forth. It would be a one-sided conception indeed to regard laws as the minimum of moral precepts.

One thing seems clear at the outset : in the case of legal obligations, we have to deal with precepts of a stricter and more *compulsory* nature than moral duties. It is obvious that in many cases the breach of a moral obligation does not directly involve material retribution, except perhaps in the form of loss of good opinion. Many a rascal takes his way through life without being made to answer for his sins if he takes care not to infringe the prescriptions of the law. It remains to be seen on what grounds this narrower sphere of legal compulsion is marked off.

CHAPTER II

1. WHEN we speak of a minimum of moral order and of moral rules as contents of law, we imply a principle which has been widely used for the purpose of defining law, namely, the principle of *coercion*. If a minimum of duties is considered as necessary for the existence of society, it must be obtained at all costs, and, if necessary, by the exertion of force. Many jurists hold therefore that law is an *enforceable* rule of conduct, in opposition to ethical rules of conduct, which are based on voluntary submission. This line of distinction has the merit of being simple and clear : let us see whether it leads to an exhaustive delimitation. The doctrine asserts, when stated more fully, that every legal rule falls into two parts : first, a *command*, stating the legal requirement; second, a *sanction* providing that if the command is not obeyed, force will be employed against the recalcitrant person. Force may be used in different ways : sometimes in the form of *execution ;* here the

act which the individual refuses to perform
is done against his will by the executive
officers of the law : thus if a man refuses to
pay a debt, the sheriff will take his money
or his furniture to satisfy the creditor.   Sometimes instead of a direct recovery or execution,
the person injured is allowed to claim *damages*,
as in the case of a breach of promise of
marriage or of injury to reputation through
libel.   Sometimes the sanction operates by
way of *punishment ;* a person who has stolen
a purse or broken into a house and abstracted
valuable property will be put into prison
whether the objects stolen or abstracted are
recoverable or not.   Lastly, the sanction may
consist in the fact that unless certain rules
are observed, an intended result cannot be
achieved.   If a person desires to make a
will, but disregards the law which requires
that such an instrument, to be valid, must be
attested by at least two witnesses, his wishes
as to the disposal of his property after death
will have no legal effect.   It may be said,
therefore, that this legal rule is supported by
the sanction of *nullity.*

If the object of law is to coerce people into
submission to certain rules, the question
inevitably arises : who is to wield the power

of coercion and to formulate rules provided
with the sanction of force ? An attempt to
answer this question is supplied by a commonly accepted definition of law, which runs
thus : *A law is a rule of conduct imposed and
enforced by the sovereign.* This definition
proceeds historically from the famous teaching
of Hobbes. He contended that men are by
nature enemies one to another, and that the
original state of mankind was a war of every
one against every one else. The intolerable
violence and anxiety of such a state was
removed by a complete renunciation on the
part of all individuals of their personal
freedom of action and by the creation of an
artificial being, *i.e.* the State, the Leviathan
in whose body every one is merged as a
particle or member, and whose sovereign will
governs every individual with unrestricted
authority. Hobbes lived at the time of the
great rebellion of the seventeenth century,
and the fierce conflicts of the Civil War
imbued him with a craving for order at any
price. He thought the best means of securing
this order was to submit to the despotic rule
of a monarch. But the absolute power of a
Parliament could be made to satisfy the
definition equally well. It has, for instance,

been said of the Parliament of England that it may do anything except turn a man into a woman, or *vice versa*. It is not the manner in which laws are elaborated, but their origin in the will of the persons possessed of public authority that is material to the theory in question. Hobbes' teaching was accepted by Austin, and, through Austin, by most English jurists. Nor are Continental writers wanting to support it. As for customary law, which is generally supposed to grow slowly out of public opinion, jurists who follow Hobbes and Austin account for it by saying that so far as it has any legal application custom must be accepted by the State. The objection that English common law is to a great extent created not by direct commands of the government, but by pronouncements of the judges, has been met by a modification of Austin's formula : " Law is the aggregate of rules recognized and acted on by courts of justice." But this modification does not change the fundamental principle of the doctrine, since it is clear that courts of justice derive their binding force from the State. The direct purpose for which judges act is, after all, the application of law, and therefore they cannot be said to exercise

independent legislative functions. A definition of law starting from their action would
therefore be somewhat like the definition of
a motor-car as a vehicle usually driven by a
chauffeur. The difference between the decree
of an absolute monarch, a statute elaborated
by Parliament, and a legal principle formulated
by judges, is technical and not fundamental :
all three proceed from the authority of a
sovereign. We shall have to treat of the
action of the courts at some length when we
come to consider the sources of law.

Let us now turn back to the original and
simpler definition : " Law is a rule of conduct
imposed and enforced by the sovereign." The
application of the theory may be illustrated
as follows :

There is my individual will, A, which I
should naturally follow if left entirely free.
But as there are numbers of other individual
wills, B, C, D, etc., some one predominant
will must intervene to regulate all these
divergent tendencies. A general compromise
must be effected and one sovereign will, say
X, set up. It may be that I am in a position
to occupy this vantage-ground, and in so far
my will, A, will be equal to X : thus the will
of a Cromwell or of a Napoleon was the will

of the State to which all other private wills had to conform. It is to be noted that the theory approaches law only from its formal side. It does not admit of any examination of the contents of legal propositions or of any inquiry into the character of the political power assumed to be the sovereign authority in the State. Law is a vehicle which may carry any kind of goods. A harsh, unjust enactment is as valid a rule as the most righteous law.

2. It is not difficult to discern the weak points of this doctrine. Surely, as has been urged by Sir H. Maine, the legal process cannot wait until a community has definitely established sovereign authority before it will recognize the existence of laws. There have been and there still are many political combinations among barbaric or half-civilized nations in which it would be impossible to ascertain exactly where sovereignty resides and whether we have to deal with a state, a tribe, a society under religious authority, or a society under concurrent authorities. How shall we apply Austin's formula to the Jews ruled by the Talmud, or to the mediæval nations of Western Europe distracted by their allegiance to King or Emperor on the one

c

side, and to the Pope on the other ? It will not help us to seek refuge in the contention that all these antiquities are of small moment in comparison with the great scientific jurisprudence of the modern State. Some of the most fundamental of our laws—*e.g.* those which regulate marriage, succession, testaments, land tenure, etc.—were evolved during this very period : that is why legal historians have so much to do with the study of antiquity. Indeed, I wonder what meaning ought to be attached, from the Austinian point of view, to a body of rules like the Canon Law—surely a sufficiently important department of legal study ? We cannot disregard the roots of legal institutions merely because they happen to be embedded in antiquity. But it is not only in ancient societies that we find legal rules which cannot be considered as the commands of a political sovereign : the same is often true to-day. For instance, it would be rather difficult to say where sovereignty, in the sense of habitual predominance, resides in a modern commonwealth like that of the United States of America. Not in Congress, because its enactments may be overruled by the Supreme Court as being contrary to the Constitution. Not in the Supreme Court, because its decisions are judicial and not governmental. Not in the people at large, because it is not a juridical, but a social and historical entity. Not in the Conventions for the reform of the Constitution, because they operate only on very exceptional occasions and are fettered in making their decisions by very restrictive rules as to majorities : and a sovereign trammelled in this way would be a contradiction in terms. The truth seems to be that the basis of law is provided not by one-sided command, but by agreement. Again, there exist within states many social bodies which possess a certain autonomy. Since the Reformation and the partial separation of Church and State, political sovereigns have to a great extent been obliged to accept the legal organization of Churches as established facts. The Church of England has been reformed outwardly by Acts of Parliament, but he would be a bold man who would assert that its external organization is entirely due to the decrees of the political sovereign. English ecclesiastical institutions certainly owe a great deal both to the Canon Law of Catholicism and to the Church organizations of Luther and Calvin. And what of the religious groups which do not " conform " ?

Is their position to be defined merely from the point of view of legal tolerance? As a matter of fact concessions have been made repeatedly to communities which have exerted the strongest possible discipline over their members, who have strenuously maintained it even in opposition to the commands of the political sovereign. The formation of autonomous spheres of law within the Churches is only one example of a widespread process. Local circles as well as professional unions may create separate rules of law; the mediæval law of Germany, for instance, was particularly wealthy in examples of such growths : there were special laws of the peasantry, of the townspeople, of crafts and guilds, of feudal societies, etc., and the dependence of all these formations on the superior law of principalities and of the empire was very lax. In England, such particularistic tendencies never got the upper hand, but still the customs of rural townships and boroughs arose from a kind of municipal autonomy and had to be recognized to a large extent by early common law. Nowadays municipal by-laws, statutes and customs of corporations, associations and trade unions of all sorts arise in abundance. They are, of course, subordinated to the laws

LEGAL RULES 37

of the kingdom as interpreted by royal
courts, but the hierarchy of legal validity
does not affect their origin and contents ;
they are produced not by the Commonwealth,
but by societies included in it; they have
their own sanctions (fines, curtailment of
privileges, exclusion); and the ultimate compromise with the law of the Commonwealth
is at bottom the outcome of a struggle for
power between central and local authorities.
The results may differ in various epochs, and
it is by no means certain that after a period
of gradual centralization of law by the State,
a movement in the opposite direction of local
and professional autonomy may not set in.

If the notion of sovereignty contained in
Austin's definition does not bear close scrutiny,
no more does the rule of conduct, as understood by him and by his followers. It is
essentially a *command;* and it may well be
asked whether law is binding only on persons
who receive the command or on those who
give it as well. The second part of every
legal rule, its sanction, is an appeal to force.
In the forging of the links of a chain of
sanctions, it is contended, we must come to
a point when arbitrary power remains master
of the ground. A Parliament is manifestly not

subject to the punitive action of the Courts; and in the same way in any monarchical country, the King is not amenable to law, " can do no wrong." If coercion be the essence of law, then law is binding only on subjects and on subordinates, while the highest persons in the State are above and outside the law.

But if this is so, why should common opinion lay so much stress on the opposition between right and might? And why should jurists trouble about Constitutional Law? Evidently what is binding on the subject by the strength of ultimate physical coercion seems to be binding on the sovereign by the strength of a moral sanction : even if the King can do no wrong in the sense that he is not amenable to punishment by his own Courts, yet he is bound to respect the laws, because he has recognized them and pledged his faith to follow them.

The German Emperor, for instance, is enjoined by cl. 17 of the Constitution of the Empire to promulgate laws enacted by the Reichstag and confirmed by him; he is forbidden by cl. 11, 2 to declare war without the consent of the Reichstag; he is bound by cl. 12 and 13 to summon the Reichstag every year, etc. But suppose he neglected to promulgate a law, or declared war on his own authority, or declined to summon the Reichstag to its yearly session. All these acts would obviously be done in infringement of legal rules, and yet there would be no direct coercion available against the head of the State.

These objections ought to make us realize that law has to be considered not merely from the point of view of its enforcement by the Courts : it depends ultimately on *recognition*. Such recognition is a distinctly legal fact, although the enforcement of a recognized rule may depend on moral restraint, the fear of public opinion, or, eventually, the fear of a popular rising.

Another difficulty arises from the position of international law. There is a set of rules recognized by the most powerful and civilized commonwealths of mankind and productive of innumerable consequences in practice ; and yet the element of direct coercion is absent from them. There is no other coercive force to ensure the maintenance of the rule that the Geneva Cross protects a hospital from destruction, or that Dum-dum bullets cannot be used in warfare, than the respect of civilized communities for public opinion and for their own honour, as far as it is pledged by the fact of their having signed certain conventions. It may even happen that when very material interests intervene, many obvious rules and customs of international law are infringed; thus the rule that a state should not attack powers with whom it is at peace was infringed by Great Britain when Copenhagen was bombarded in 1807 for fear that the Danish fleet should be used by Napoleon. Again, Austria-Hungary the other day turned the occupation of Bosnia and Herzegovina into annexation without obtaining leave from the signatories of the Treaty of Berlin. By reason of this absence of coercive sanction some jurists refuse to international law the attributes of law properly so-called, and look upon it merely as a form of positive morality. This is, however, going much too far; international legal rules carry a great weight of practical authority; and in their actual content, they are exactly similar to ordinary laws, and in many cases have nothing to do with ethics. Take the rule that a state exercises jurisdiction over the high seas within three miles from its shores : how does this differ from an ordinary rule of constitutional law ?

Clearly not in its essence, though perhaps in the manner of its formulation and enforcement. The inference seems to be that international law is truly a department of law so far as law is a declaration of right, but that it is peculiar as regards the element of sanction. In this respect it may be called *imperfect*, or less than perfect law.

One more characteristic feature should be mentioned in this connection. As regards the enforcement of civil liabilities, law is powerless to provide a sanction so complete as to amount to a guarantee against injury and loss : it can do no more than intervene on behalf of the party claiming a right, but whether the claim can be satisfied or not will in numberless cases depend on circumstances over which law has no control. Suppose a Court has awarded heavy damages as the result of a collision in the road by which you have suffered bodily injury; the party against whom the decision is awarded turns out to be a person of small means entirely incapable of paying the compensation. Is not the legal rule provided with incomplete sanction ? Or take the instance of the responsibility of agents of a Trade Union for damages inflicted by illegal interference with your right to hire workmen; are you sure their personal liability would be an adequate guarantee against your suffering heavy losses in the event of a strike? Hardly; and yet the rules laid down by law in such cases would be emphatic and clear, though provided with insufficient sanction.

The upshot of this discussion of the element of direct coercion seems to be that, though commonly present, it is not absolutely necessary to constitute a legal rule; and that while we may look upon it as the most convenient means for enforcing law, we cannot regard it as the essence of legal relations. Clearly it has to be supplemented by restraints based on personal recognition and on public opinion. Therefore it is impossible to confine law within the terms of such a purely formal definition as is involved in its consideration as a set of commands, quite apart from any contents. Law aims at right and justice, however imperfectly it may achieve this aim in particular cases. If we omitted this attribute from our definition, we should find it very difficult to draw the line between a law and any kind of arbitrary order as to conduct, *e.g.* the levying of regular blackmail by a criminal association. There must be a certain balance between justice and force in every system of law; and therefore it is impossible to give a definition of law based exclusively on coercion by the State.

8. An important step is made when attention is turned from the means to the end, from compulsion to the substance of legal rules. What is the end for the sake of which human beings submit to constraint? Kant came to the conclusion that the aim of law is *freedom*, and that the fundamental process of law is the adjustment of one's freedom to that of every other member of the community. This principle was expressed by him in the famous sentence : " Act in such a way that your liberty shall accord with that of all and of each one." The notion of freedom, however, was not happily selected, since it is obvious that the adjustment effected by law must consist in the curtailment of individual freedom, and freedom, as usually understood, merely opens the way for possible action, but does not indicate the course action should take.

One of the leading nineteenth century jurists, Ihering, found the end of law in the *delimitation of interests*.[1] Freedom to exert

[1] Ihering himself was mainly concerned with the nature of *rights* : as to legal rules, the consequences of his doctrine have been summarized by Korkunov, *The Theory of Law* (Hastings' translation, p. 52).

one's will seemed meaningless to him : all
our actions are suggested by a striving
towards some kind of value, either physical
or moral, and the responsible task of the
law supported by the State is to apportion
individual spheres of interests and to uphold
the repartition thus effected. It seems, however, that by making the State a judge of
conflicting interests, Ihering has saddled it
with a heavy responsibility which is not
necessarily implied in the notion of law, and
is easily liable to misconception. Neither the
State nor its law can assume the impossible
task of influencing all the interests involved
in social life and of guiding individuals in
the selection and management thereof. The
State may for various reasons pick out some
particular spheres of interests for special
supervision—say public health or education.
But it is not bound to do so in all directions
merely because it wields the force of law,
What it *is* bound to do is to see that the wills
of the members of the community do not
clash while striving towards the attainment
of their ends. It has, as it were, to lay down
and enforce the rule of the road on which
individuals are moving. Some civilized states
have never gone further than this; other

governments have undertaken to solve or to
assist in solving economic and cultural problems; but such an extension of aim does not
commit us to a definition of law which would
make social policy the essential element of
legal arrangements.   An energetic social policy
is, after all, only a manifestation of the will
of the State as a political corporation and, as
such, it constitutes one of the objects for legal
delimitation and   protection—but only one
among many.   It is true that in some instances—*e.g.* minors, idiots, spendthrifts—
law steps in to protect the interests of the
individual, while at the same time it recognizes that his will is insufficient to make his
acts legally valid.   But is not this another
way of saying that the individual will, before
it can claim recognition and protection from
the law of the State, has to justify itself as
one which is independent, reasonable and
complete ?   When one of these attributes is
lacking, law has to supply substitutes or
complements in the shape of guardians and
curators, just as it may have to recognize
representatives and trustees.   It still remains
true that the decision as to interests is left
to some will or other, either natural or
artificial.

4. Let us, then, start from Ihering's definition and carry it one step further by substituting *volition* for *interest*. We may take it for granted that human wills pursue their several interests when free to exert themselves. The problem consists in allowing such an exercise of each personal will as is compatible with the exercise of other wills. As soon as a rule of the road is established to prevent collisions between persons moving in the same thoroughfare, a legal rule comes into existence : it may be reached by agreement or by custom, or imposed by higher authority, but its legal essence consists in the fact that it is recognized as a rule of conduct by the travellers on the road. The fact that it may sometimes be ignored or infringed does not abolish it if it is usually respected. Notice that it is not a rule of morality, but of convenience. It springs not from kindness, or generosity, or honesty, but from the view that one's own interests are connected with those of others. It may assume all the aspects of a law imposed by the State and serve as a basis for the award of damages and the punishment of negligence : but in its simplest expression it is an agreement to drive to the left or to the right, as the case may be, when meeting

another vehicle; in other words, it is a limitation of one's freedom of action for the sake of avoiding collision with others. The rule of the road leaves every person moving under its direction severely to himself, but in social life, as we know, men have not only to avoid collisions, but to arrange co-operation in all sorts of ways, and the one common feature of all these forms of co-operation is the limitation of individual wills in order to achieve a common purpose. Now, what is limitation for one will is *power* for another. When I restrict my range of action out of consideration for another person, or for a body of men, or for a common undertaking, I concede power to this other person, or to the body of men, or to the managers of the common undertaking, and increase their range of actions and the power of their wills. And in reality the whole of society is built up by such combinations of social power under the direction of legal rules. I think we may say that the aim of law is to regulate the attribution and exercise of power over persons and things in social intercourse.

Let us dwell for a moment on the meaning of the term " power." The word is of course used sometimes in the material sense : when

we speak of water-power or electric-power or
horse-power, we think of forces of nature as
far as they can be subordinated to human
volition; but any combination creating social
forces is also commonly described as power.
In this sense, we speak not only of political
authority, but of all forms of juridical compulsion. The " power " conferred on an
attorney or a plenipotentiary, for example,
appears as a delegation within a specified
range of the influence exerted by the principal.
Or we may take an illustration of the use of
the term " power " in the sense of a legal
range of action from the practice of " testamentary disposition "—*i.e.* the making of
wills.   When a person makes a will in accordance with the rules established by law, he
expresses wishes which will be upheld by the
community at a time when he, the testator,
will be dead and unable to exercise any
physical power whatever.   In this way, the
attribution of power to a testator is clearly
dependent on the authority of the law-making
community.   Thus it may be said that all
forms of social combination are set in motion
by power distributed according to a certain
order.   If the limitations of will which condition power are something more than casual

devices, and are determined in a constant manner, rules arise which are legal in their essence, even apart from the amount of constraint which they may contain. When two persons sit down to play a game of cards, they subordinate their individual wills to the rules of the game, and if one of the players chooses to disregard those rules, the other will remonstrate and perhaps abandon the game. From the technical point of view this result may be considered as an instance of the sanction of nullity. The presence of a superior authority is not necessary for the existence of such a rule, and the same may be said. of the rules governing many other social groups.

In defining law we have to start from a given society, not necessarily from a state, because every human society is bound to set up certain laws in order that the individuals composing it should not go each his own way instead of co-operating towards the formation of a higher unity. A casual concourse of individuals—a group of passers-by listening to a preacher in Hyde Park—is not a society. But if a number of persons agree to act in a certain way when they meet, say to assemble on certain days to worship together, they form a society for a definite purpose, and

D

must submit to certain rules laid down in one way or another if they wish to achieve that purpose. The individual ceases to be quite free, and has to co-ordinate his actions with those of his fellows, while the purpose for which the union is formed provides the whole community with an aim which has to be achieved by decisions similar to the acts of will of a live being. This collective will is, so far as the society is concerned, superior to the will of any individual member. A joint stock company, a learned society, a city corporation, a county, a Free Church, or the Catholic Church, are societies with corporate aims and wills. They enact laws regulating the conduct of their members. A state is a society of the same kind, although its aims are more complex—protection of citizens, dominion over territory, judicial power, economic or cultural policy, etc. The government and the laws of a commonwealth, although towering over all other forms of association and possibly regulating and re-stricting them, are still essentially of the same kind as the rules which hold together a private union or a local body.

Laws are made to be obeyed and enforced. The wills and actions of members of a society

are not regulated merely by convenience, or
voluntary resolve, or habit, or inclination,
or sense of duty, but by social necessity.
Unless the wills and actions of the members
fit together like the cogs of a machine, or
rather like the organs of a living body, the
society cannot exist. A certain amount of
irregularity may have to be tolerated in any
human contrivance, but should every member
allow himself to act as if his adhesion were
merely casual and voluntary, the association
would not work, and, instead of promoting
its distinctive aims, would be distracted by
the vagaries of its members. As far as these
aims go, the will of the community is a
superior authority, and therefore the rules
imposed by it ought to have a binding force.
That is why in most cases such rules are
provided with sanctions, with threats of
unpleasant consequences in case of infringement : fines, payment of damages, temporary
or perpetual exclusion, deprivation of spiritual
boons (*e.g.* of the Sacrament), excommunication or curse in the case of religious communities, imprisonment or even death in
case of the infringement of laws of a state.
The enforcement of laws by execution or by
the infliction of punishment is not, however,

indispensable for the constitution of a legal rule. It is sufficient that a sanction should be present in most cases, though on exceptional occasions there may be a miscarriage of justice in this respect: a debtor may be insolvent, a criminal may escape. Certain laws again would lack direct sanction and would depend for their observance on recognition by the persons concerned. Altogether we must remember that sooner or later we come to a point where law is obeyed not on account of material compulsion, but for other reasons—in consequence of reasonable acceptance, or instinctive conformity, or habit, or absence or organized resistance. If it were not so, how could commonwealths and legal systems exist? The number of people who can resort to command and coercion is generally infinitesimal in comparison with the number of those who have to be led and eventually coerced. It is only as long as criminals are in a minority and as long as the nation at large remains law-abiding that law can have its way. This means that it is not the material possibility of coercion so much as the mental habit of recognizing rules imposed by social authority that is decisive in regard to the existence of laws.

5. Laws are rules, but what is a rule in the juridical sense ? A rule may be defined as a direction as to conduct. Each of these terms requires special examination.

(*a*) A *direction* is not necessarily a command : it includes a declaration of what is right and what is wrong. A signpost on your way does not command you to go to the right or to the left, but it tells you that if you go to the right you will reach place A, which we may suppose to be your destination; if you go to the left you will reach place B, that is, you will go wrong as far as your aim is concerned. Even so in law : there are a number of legal rules which do not go further than to state the conditions which society considers to be necessary if a person wishes to give effect to a certain purpose. If I want to sell my house, I have to do it by means of a written instrument couched in a certain form. Should I attempt to sell it in another way, say by delivering it to the purchaser before witnesses, the transaction will have no legal effect and I shall not be able to claim the price agreed upon. I ought to have followed the declaration of the Statute of Frauds, s. 4, which is a law provided with a sanction of nullity. On the other hand, there are many laws which carry a punitive sanction. This means that the society which imposes them considers them binding not only in regard to the mutual relations of its members, but also in regard to its own interests directly or indirectly. If a person who has made an invalid sale insists on keeping money on the assumption that the sale was a regular one, the State will take this money from him and eventually punish him for defying the authority of a declaration made by the legislative organ of the State. A citizen submits to a legal rule not as to an arbitrary command, but as to a declaration or right which is supported by the authority of the Commonwealth or of a given association.

(b) Legal rules are intended to direct the *conduct* of men, that is, their actions and outward behaviour : they do not aim at controlling men's thoughts and desires. The object of law is to ensure social order, and therefore it has to regulate the relations between men, and not their inner consciousness. The latter task has been attempted sometimes, *e.g.* in prosecutions for heresy, but the motives in such cases have not been legal. What is wrong from our present point of view in such prosecutions is not the fact of proceeding against opinions considered to be false, but the manner in which such proceedings were taken. A Church has a perfect right to condemn opinions which it deems to be false or immoral; it may proceed against the holders of such opinions by its own peculiar means—by spiritual penances and ultimately by excommunication. But the extradition of the culprit to the secular arm, the attempt to enforce right creed by the help of the police and of the hangman, are unjustifiable from our present point of view.

At the same time conduct in more or less advanced societies is not considered as a series of purely external phenomena. It is not the same kind of occurrence as the fall of a stone or a stroke of lightning. It is the product of will, and the will is called into action by motives. This being so, modern jurisprudence takes care to distinguish whether conduct is the result of ordinary consciousness and reason, or is brought about by agencies which deprive it of this deliberate character. Lunatics kill men every now and then, and are tried for homicide; but if examination has shown the deed to be the result of a disordered mind, it is considered in the same light as a phenomenon

of nature, and does not involve criminal responsibility. The slayer will be sent to an
asylum or otherwise put under restraint,
but this is a measure of precaution, not of
punishment; it may happen that he will be
set at liberty again after recovery. In the
same way an action that would be a misdeed
if done by an adult is merely a misfortune
when done by a child : a boy under seven
could not be found guilty of arson for setting
fire to a haystack.

Then again, certain actions are judged
differently by law according to the intention
behind them : wilful homicide is legally very
different from manslaughter, and the burning
down of a house through negligence does not
involve the same consequences to the person
responsible for it as premeditated arson.
Thus we perceive that legal doctrine considers conduct as the product of a reasonable
will, or rather of a will guided by normal
reason. The interference of the law may be
called for, however, not merely after the
event, when a misfortune has happened :
preventive measures are also contemplated
by law; insane people are not only put under
supervision and restraint in order that they
may not do damage to their neighbours, but

they are provided with curators in order that they shall not squander their fortune or employ it in an unreasonable way. The further development of these views belongs to the doctrines of responsibility, liability, civil capacity, etc. : I merely wish for the present to show that the will and the mind are not left outside the consideration of law, but that its rules take them into account for the sake of estimating conduct and only in so far as they influence conduct.

The above simple illustrations afford a clue which will be found useful in another set of cases, namely, those in which legal rules aim at giving effect to the intention of the individual. Apart from the question of rights and duties created by an obligation, it is necessary in modern law that the obligation should be a matter of consent, that is, of free-will. Intimidation, corruption, fraud, in some cases mistake as to facts, will invalidate a formally complete obligation. In the same way important inquiries as to freedom of resolve and soundness of mind arise in cases of testamentary dispositions. In every way human conduct is estimated in connection with the will expressed in it, though it is the conduct and not the inner consciousness of man that the law takes as its starting-point.

6. To sum up: we have seen that legal rules contain declarations as to right and wrong conduct, formulated in accordance with the will of a society and intended to direct the wills of its members. Such declarations will be supported by all means at the disposal of the society which has laid them down, ranging from physical coercion to nullification and exclusion. This being so, law is clearly distinguishable from morality. The object of law is the submission of the individual to the will of organized society, while the tendency of morality is to subject the individual to the dictates of his own conscience. The result has to be achieved in the former case by a combination of wills, co-ordinating them with each other. At the same time it is clear that in every healthy society laws regulating the attribution of power ought to be in harmony with recognized moral precepts: and substantial discrepancies in this respect are sure to produce mischief in the shape of divided opinions and uncertainty of conduct.

Within the aggregate produced by this combination of wills each component will

must have its range of play and power.
Therefore law may be defined as a *set of rules
imposed and enforced by a society with regard
to the attribution and exercise of power over
persons and things.* A certain hierarchy of wills
has to be established : taking the simplest
case, one person obtains power over another
in the sense that he can direct the will of the
other and make it serve his own ends, or a
common end. Such ends may be exceedingly various, comprising, for instance, the
use of land or goods, services, profits, etc.
The common feature, however, in all these
cases would be the *power* of a certain will to
bind others. The proposed definition of law
seems to fit the different historical stages of
development. It covers the case of primitive
legal rules which had to be largely enforced by
self-help, as well as that of the highly complex
commonwealths of the present day which
strive to provide complete systems of legal
remedies and State sanctions. It embraces
the working of by-laws, customs and autonomous ordinances, as well as that of the
common law and of elaborate parliamentary
enactments. It makes room for the binding
force of Constitutional and of International
Law. It takes account of criminal and of

private law, of punishment and of nullity. Its principal title to recognition consists in the fact that it lays stress on the purpose of law rather than on the means by which law is enforced.

CHAPTER III

LEGAL RIGHTS AND DUTIES

1. WE have already noticed the highly significant fact that in most European languages the term for law is identical with the term for right. The Latin *jus*, the German *Recht*, the Italian *diritto*, the Spanish *derecho*, the Slavonic *pravo* point both to the legal rule which binds a person and the legal right which every person claims as his own. Such coincidences cannot be treated as mere chance, or as a perversion of language likely to obscure the real meaning of words. On the contrary, they point to a profound connection between the two ideas implied, and it is not difficult to see why expressions like *jus* and *Recht* face both ways : it may be said that on the one hand all private rights are derived from legal order, while, on the other hand, legal order is in a sense the aggregate of all the rights co-ordinated by it. We can hardly define a right better than by saying that it is the

range of action assigned to a particular will within the social order established by law. Just because every person under the rule of law divests himself of an unlimited liberty of action, a certain liberty of action limited in extent and direction is conceded and guaranteed to him by right. A right therefore supposes a potential exercise of power in regard to things or persons. It enables the subject endowed with it to bring, with the approval of organized society, certain things or persons within the sphere of action of his will. When a man claims something as his right, he claims it as *his own* or as *due to him*. Naturally enough, his first claims concern his own life and limbs, and the Commonwealth concedes the claim by pledging itself to protect his person. It has not always been so : in ancient times, the claim led only to a declaration of right on the part of a tribal society, while for actual protection a freeman had to look to his own strength and to that of his kinsmen or fellows. Next comes the claim to personal freedom from arbitrary imprisonment or interference with one's movements. Closely connected with this is the right to be protected from unauthorized intrusion into one's home. It is well known what historical struggles have been produced by these elementary claims, and how imperfectly they are realized even nowadays in some communities which deem themselves civilized. Rights to free thought, free conscience, free belief and free speech are asserted on the same ground of personal freedom, though they are often counteracted by considerations of public safety and public morality. And besides the protection of material existence, in more or less advanced communities men claim as by right protection of their reputation and honour : law gradually displaces self-help in preventing and punishing insult and slander.

While this first group of rights clusters round the idea of *personality*, a second group is formed round the idea of *property*. We consider as our own not only our body, our home and our honour, but also the proceeds of conquest and labour (including mental work, *e.g.* of authors, inventors, artists, etc.). It rests with the State to determine the rules as to the accumulation, disposal and protection of property. One of the most important developments of the right to property consists in the transfer of this right to successors.

No human being stands entirely isolated in this world; every one is more or less affected by the ties of the family and of the State, and perhaps of many intermediate organizations. The exercise of the will in these relations leads to various rights of *authority* and corresponding duties. It is obvious that the rights of a father, of a husband, of a guardian, and also their duties in regard to children, wives, wards, etc., arise from this source. The status of the citizen, denizen, civil officer, soldier, foreigner, also give rise to rights and duties of a personal character.

A fourth group is formed by the rights derived from obligations based on agreements between persons possessed of the capacity to enter into such agreements; a fifth by rights arising out of wrongs committed by other persons, for instance, rights to compensation for damage inflicted by trespassers, etc. And lastly there appears the complex system of rights exercised by the State and its officers in their public capacity, the rights giving power to judges, magistrates, administrative officers, commanders, and embracing both their executive functions and their jurisdiction in criminal and civil cases.

The above enumeration is intended merely to give a general view of the powers claimed under the sway of legal rules by the members of the Commonwealth in their divers capacity and combinations.

2. Let us now pass to a closer analysis of the notion of legal right and of its counterpart, legal duty. The best way to realize the nature of rights is to observe their exercise in social intercourse. Legal intercourse runs parallel to social intercourse : one cannot be thought of without the other. In social intercourse most varied relations are created and dissolved every moment; men love and hate, help and hinder, educate and exploit each other, join in conversation, in business, in literary and scientific work. But in the legal forms of this intercourse, relations assume always one aspect; they are varieties of the fundamental correspondence between right and duty which constitutes legal power. Men either *claim* or *owe* in their legal relations. For example, A exerts a right, that is, A legally has the power to require from B, or from B, C, D, etc., that he or they shall act or forbear to act in a certain way. If A is entitled to assert such a right, B, C, D, etc., or any one of them, is bound to discharge certain duties—to do something, or to abstain from doing something. To give one or two concrete instances : A, being the master, has

E

a right over B, the servant, in regard to **X,**
certain services. The relation may be expressed in a typical formula. A (subject)
requires (predicate) certain services from B
(object). Or, if we turn the sentence from
the active to the passive, B (subject of duty)
owes (predicate) certain services to A (object).
In legal relations of this kind A and B are
both subjects : one of a right, the other of
a duty, which may be construed as the passive
side of a right. The predicate in active
sentences is " requires " : in passive sentences
" owes, is bound to." Lastly, the service
required appears as the material contents of
the right and of the duty; grammatically and
juridically they are the object of the predicate, providing it with a concrete sub-
stratum. There can be no empty rights and
no indefinite duties. Still, it is to be noticed
that according to our analysis the introduction
of the thing required is merely a means to
provide the relations between A and B with
some material : it does not create a relation
between A and X (service) or between B
and X; the legal relation exists exclusively
between A and B.

A similar relation is expressed in the
sentence : " B, the servant, requires A, the

master, to pay his wages." When inverted
the relation would be expressed by the
sentence : " A (the master), owes wages to B
(the servant)."

A different type is presented by a sentence
like this : A (the landowner), requires B,
C, D, etc.—every one—to abstain from interference with a piece of land (Y). Here the
subject of the duty is not one determinate
person, but any person likely to interfere
with A's right. A is sometimes said to
exercise his right "against all the world ";
as it is expressed in Roman legal terminology,
A has a " right over the thing " (*jus in rem*).
This way of treating the relation is quite
acceptable from one point of view, but it is
not the only possible nor the necessary one.
The case lends itself quite as well to the
construction already adopted by us. The
right of A in regard to an estate of land may
be conveniently analysed as a legal relation
between A and B, C, D and an indefinite
number of other persons, who are excluded
by the exercise of A's right from interfering
with the estate. Their duty is one of ab-
stention ; A's right is one of prohibition, which
makes him exclusive owner and enables him
to use the estate as he chooses. The advantage

of such a construction of the right is that it
enables us to treat it from the point of view
of the personal relations between the members
of a society, which are at bottom the only
relations the law can regulate. The notion
of property or exclusive ownership which we
have to fit into the legal frame in the case
under discussion is, after all, a notion entirely
produced by the regulation of intercourse
between citizens. It is not a natural function
in itself, like tilling or depasturing soil or
building on land. Therefore the right of
ownership is, strictly speaking, quite as much
a personal right—the right of one person
against other persons—as a right to service,
or a lease. It may be convenient for certain
purposes to speak of rights over things, but
in reality there can be only rights *in respect
of* things *against* persons, in the same way
as there are rights in respect of the use of
one's labour or in respect of the use of somebody else's labour. Relations and intercourse
arise exclusively between live beings; but
goods as well as ideas are the object and the
material of such relations; and when a right
of ownership in a watch or a piece of land is
granted to me by law, this means not only
that the seller has entered into a personal

obligation to deliver those things to me, but also that every other person will be bound to recognize them as mine—an artificial notion created and insisted upon for the sake of legal intercourse.

It is also to be noticed as a peculiarity of the second type of juridical relations that the subject of right cannot be converted into a subject of duty and *vice versa*, as in the first type. But the right conceded to the individual in this case is matched by similar rights vested in other members of the community. If A excludes B, C and D from his property, B has the same power of exclusion in regard to A, C and D, C in regard to A, B and D, etc.

A third type of juridical relation is constituted by the rights of the Commonwealth itself as expressed in its legal rules. The Commonwealth, A, is the subject of the right in this relation; it requires (predicate) the obedience of citizens to its laws (object); this obedience provides the conception of duty with material contents, and therefore forms the object of right. If the relation is de-scribed from the point of view of duty, the citizens would evidently appear as subjects of the duty, with corresponding changes in predicate and object.   The inverted or passive statement of the relation would be, the citizens (B) owe obedience to the Commonwealth in respect of its laws.

Thus the aggregate of legal rules imposed by a state or other society appears as the material complement or object of the society's right to the obedience of its members.   Every single legal rule may be thought of as one of the bulwarks or boundaries erected by society in order that its members shall not collide with each other in their actions.   Not to speak of such fundamental guarantees as the commandments " Thou shalt not kill," " Thou shalt not steal," " Thou shalt not commit adultery," every legal rule appears as a necessary adjunct to some relation of social intercourse, and it is often difficult to say whether the rule precedes the rights and duties involved in the relation, or *vice versa.* From the historical point of view, the latter alternative seems the more probable.   When merchants land on a coast inhabited by a savage tribe and barter beads for ivory, customs of exchange develop before there is any authority capable of framing rules as to the contract of barter.   Dying persons must have often disposed of their goods on their death-bed before the law of testamentary succession took shape. But we are not engaged now in tracing historical sequences in the development of rights and rules. It may suffice to notice that both these sides of law stand in constant cross-relations one to another. In a full survey of the matter, equal stress ought to be laid on rights and duties : but in practice, rights are chiefly insisted upon in private law, duties in public law.

3. The subjects of rights and duties in modern law are necessarily persons, that is, living human beings. As soon as such a being is conceived the law recognizes its personality and assigns certain rights to it. Even the embryo in its mother's womb is protected in its existence : to destroy it is a criminal offence; certain rights of property may be affected by its existence, *e.g.* if the father be deceased intestate, the succession may be regarded as destined for it when it comes to life : and if it comes to life only for a moment, the further course of intestate succession will depend on that fact, though the sole indication of actual life has been a faint cry or a momentary palpitation of the heart. In such a case it is by legal process

that personality is recognized and endowed with rights, and the intention of the law is clear : it wishes to make sure that the possibilities offered by nature to a living being shall be protected to the utmost against accident and foul play. On the other hand law takes good care that the rights with which it endows such embryonic beings shall remain latent or shall be exercised only by proxy until personality attains maturity of free will. Hence the well-known restrictions placed upon persons under age—wardship, etc. Even persons over age are not always considered as possessed of full powers in the exercise of their rights. Custody of the madman and the spendthrift was not unknown even to ancient law. These facts have afforded material for a theory to which I have already referred, namely, that the object of law is the protection of interests (Ihering). It is urged that it is the interests and not the will of the infant or of the feeble-minded which are taken care of. But a little reflection shows that law does not deal indiscriminately with all sorts of wills and minds, but with the normal will and mind of the average person. When, for some reason such as disease or old age, the average is not reached, the law provides substitutes and supports, but certainly does not destroy the cardinal qualification of free will. On the contrary, it sets up reasonable standards to which free wills have to conform. In any case, the notion of free personality must be regarded as a most important element in the construction of rights : for on it depend the relations between subjects and predicates in the legal sense.

4. A subject of right must be a living person, but need not be *one* person. A plurality of persons may act as a subject of right as well as a single individual. It is not unusual for a house to be owned by several co-heirs. The occupants of houses surrounding a square may enjoy the right of walking in the square in the same way as every one of them enjoys the right of walking in his own garden.

Here personality is ascribed to a plurality of unconnected individuals; but it may also be ascribed to a definitely constituted association of individuals; thus in the last example, the right to use the square may depend on the fact that certain householders are members of an association for keeping up that particular square, and their rights and duties belong **to**

them only in so far as they take part in this
association. Persons forming an association
of this kind may either act jointly or in
common, that is, they may appear as partners
with strictly defined shares, or else as par-
ticipants with undetermined rights; a commercial firm may serve as an instance of the
first kind, a club whose members have the
use of certain furnished premises of the other.
In many cases, however, the collective personality created by the association of a number
of individuals for a certain purpose consists
in a more or less complicated partnership,
that is to say, a contractual relation which
results in a certain unity of action as regards
outsiders; but when looked at from the
inside, the association consists of a number
of independent persons who have agreed to
act together.

But we have also to reckon in law with the
existence of bodies or unions which develop
a distinct personality of their own, not a
combination formed out of the individual
personalities of partners, and not dissolved by
the secession of individual members. We
cannot plunge into the intricate details of
doctrines as to corporations and associations :
what I wish to show is the effect of the legal

recognition of personality in aggregate bodies which, though composed of individuals, are considered as being one and undivided in themselves. Organic unity is often supplied to such corporations by a grant from the State : but in such cases the Commonwealth generally confirms and recognizes what has been already prepared by social intercourse. For example, historical corporations like towns or churches do not depend for their formation on express agreement or grant, but on a constant aim or purpose, such as the organization of municipal life or spiritual exercises in a certain place.

The existence of corporations gives rise to an interesting juridical problem. We began the discussion as to subjects of right by saying that they must be live human beings. How will this apply to such bodies as the City of Oxford, or Corpus Christi College ? In some respects they act like individuals : they hold property, contract loans, pay salaries, take care of buildings, carry on certain definite work, such as the sanitation of the town, or the teaching of undergraduates ; nor can they be dissolved at pleasure by their members.

It clearly would not do to consider the existence of a corporation like the City of

Oxford as a contractual association of its inhabitants. But it would not do either in the case of a corporation like a college. It would be absurd to resolve the life of Corpus Christi College into the constituent elements of the lives of the President and the Fellows of each particular year, or month, or week. The really important point evidently is that the institution remains one and distinct in spite of the constant change of individuals who from time to time act as its members. We are met by the fact that a social organization of this kind, although necessarily embodied in certain individual persons for the time being, yet leads a life of its own, as a higher being provided with its own will, its own aims and an appropriate organization to exercise the will and achieve the aims. What has been said of corporations like a city or a college is also true of organic bodies like a commonwealth or a church, which are formed not by express agreement, but by the force of circumstances. A variety modelled on the pattern of such organic corporations is presented by corporate bodies which have been created by an express grant of the State. The numerous chartered companies of English Law belong to this species.

The characteristic trait of these organic societies is thus their double life, the combined existence of the juridical organization and of the members filling its frame at each particular moment. The existence of a distinct personality may be illustrated by a kind of conundrum. If there are a hundred people assembled in a room to work out a decree of the University of Oxford, how many persons are there in the room? Not a hundred, certainly, but a hundred and one : because, besides the individuals, there is the corporate personality whose will has to be expressed. Is the existence of such more than human organizations a mere legal fiction, contrived for the purpose of linking certain persons together and introducing a principle of continuity into their acts and dealings? Many jurists have thought so, and the theory has led to most important conclusions in practice, for example, the doctrine that a corporation cannot commit tortious acts. This legal doctrine has been widely held by Continental authorities, and appears also in English cases. Thus in *Abrath* v. *North Eastern Railway Co.* (1886), Lord Bramwell said :

" I am of opinion that no action for a

malicious prosecution will lie against a corporation. . . . To maintain an action for malicious prosecution it must be shown that there was an absence of reasonable and probable cause, and that there was malice or some indirect and illegitimate motive in the prosecutor. A corporation is incapable of malice or of motive. If the whole body of shareholders were to meet and in so many words to say, ' prosecute A not because we believe him guilty, but because it will be for our interest to do it,' no action would lie against the corporation, though it would lie against the shareholders."

But judges who had to decide similar cases later on were driven to abandon Lord Bramwell's doctrine, and this for good reasons. In a 1904 case, *Citizen's Life Assurance Company* v. *Brown*, proceedings arose out of a libel contained in a circular addressed by the agent of a rival company to several persons assured in the appellant Company. Lord Lindley on appeal remarked :

" The question raised by this appeal is whether a limited Company is responsible for a libel published by one of its officers. . . ." [The facts showed (shortly) that

Fitzpatrick, in reply to the action of Brown, who had endeavoured to induce policy-holders in the Citizen's Life Assurance Company to join another in which he was interested, sent out a circular letter to these persons which was plainly defamatory; it contained statements which Fitzpatrick knew not to be true. There was evidence of express malice on the part of Fitzpatrick. It was contended that the malice with which he wrote could not be imputed to the Company].

" If it is once granted that corporations are for civil purposes to be regarded as persons, *i.e.* as principals acting by agents and servants, it is difficult to see why the ordinary doctrines of agency, and of master and servant, are not to be applied to corporations as well as to ordinary individuals.

" These doctrines have been so applied in a great variety of cases, in questions arising out of contracts, and in questions arising out of torts and frauds; and to apply them to one class of libels and to deny their application to another class of libels on the ground that malice cannot be imputed to a body corporate appears to their lordships to be contrary to sound legal principles."

In keeping with this view, Mr. Justice Darling, in *Cornford* v. *Carlton Bank* (1900) remarked :

" I am satisfied the prosecution was without reasonable and probable cause, and that the defendants were acting with malice, in the sense that they were actuated by such motives as would be malice in law, were they the motives of a private person."

This means that in modern English law the " personal " existence of a corporation is regarded not as a fiction, but as a reality. Thus a body corporate has been held to be a " respectable and responsible person " within the meaning of the usual proviso in a lease limiting a lessor's right to object to an assignment by the lessee [*Willmott* v. *London Road Car Co.* (1910)]. Though composed of many individuals, a " corporation aggregate " is deemed to be a distinct person by itself animated by the purpose which it pursues and embodies in the organization which has been framed for it.

Besides corporations expressly acknowledged by law, there is a considerable number of social formations which, as it were, hover on the borderland of corporate existence and present

some difficulties to legal analysis. Trade
unions are a conspicuous instance. They hold
and administer property, they pursue a permanent end distinct from the business aims
of their members, they are organized to
exercise influence both on their own members
and on outsiders. Yet they are not corporations, and refuse to be treated as such : and
hence the problem of liability discussed in
regard to corporations has arisen with peculiar
force in connection with the activity of trade
unions.

It is well known that recent legislation on
the subject of trade disputes (Act 1906) was
partly prompted by a desire to amend the
state of the law as declared in the famous
Taff Vale case.[1] A Railway Company sought
an injunction against the Amalgamated
Society of Railway Servants, agents and
members of which, it was complained, had
been picketing and besetting workmen who
were likely to be employed by the Railway.
It is needless for us to examine the facts of
the case, but we have to remember that the
highest legal authority of the kingdom, the
House of Lords, came to the conclusion that

[1] *Taff Vale Railway* v. *Amalgamated Society of Railway
Servants* (1901).

F

if tortious acts had been committed, the responsibility for them would fall on the Trade Union itself.

This view is in accord with what has been said before on the status of corporations, but Parliament in 1906 altered the law to the effect that Trade Unions were not to be held liable in such cases. This implies that in view of their special aims unions of this kind are given a privileged position in trade disputes : [1] for otherwise their action in the defence of labour would be hampered. These are *quasi-corporations*.

Another species of artificial persons arises when certain aggregates of rights have been instituted for a definite purpose but not attributed to any definite subject of right. Charities are in this position. If money has been left to provide for the education of poor children, or for the maintenance of a ward at a hospital, English law furnishes the machinery of administration by the institution of trustees, who act as subjects of the right, although they are responsible to the Commonwealth for the exercise of this right in the manner provided by the benefactor or testator. In Continental law the case is somewhat more complicated:

[1] See below, pp. 97, 126.

the charity is treated as a kind of union for a definite purpose, although the elements of association are wanting. Here the administrators of the charity are the subjects of the right : but the exercise of right is strictly determined by the document of foundation, and the administrators embody the will of the juridical unit as far as it is free to act in accordance with the provisions of this document. Limitations do not affect in any way the fundamental character of the right. Continental jurists have felt some difficulties as to the position of the persons who benefit by the trust : but English law, with its doctrine of trusts, makes this position easy to understand; the sick or the children whom the charity helps for the time being may be likened to the " *cestui que trust* " for whose sake the trustee administers the trust : they are beneficiaries protected by the State, but certainly not subjects of right.

When the subject is not expressly defined, when, for instance, a right of way is opened for use to every passer-by, we have the same type of legal relation as when every man is deemed to be the subject of a duty, *e.g.* every man is obliged to respect a right of ownership. Any one, B, C, D, may in such a case exercise the right and assert the corresponding claims, as often happens in regard to rights of way. But it is not impossible to make the public at large, or the State as its representative, the subject of such rights.

5. The objects of rights and duties may be of two kinds, either things, that is, material bodies which persons seek to appropriate and to use, as land, cattle, money, furniture, etc., or abstract interests, that is, claims in regard to human forces and activities, *e.g.* services, contractual obligations of all kinds, the good-will of a firm, literary or artistic productions. In a wider sense it may be said that material things are also not directly objects of rights and duties, but indirectly, as far as interests in them are allowed or recognized by law. Thus it is not actually the house which forms the object of a householder's right, but the interest he has in it, the ownership or the possession of the house. On the other hand, it is usual to class abstract interests as *incorporeal things*, just as we classify under the same grammatical head abstract nouns like courage, faith, science, and concrete nouns like chair, sword, tree. Either one or the other basis of classification may be used, provided it is followed consistently. I prefer

to speak of things and abstract realities or interests, because this terminology lays stress on the fundamental reason why every legal relation has to be constructed with the help not only of subjects of rights and duties, but also of objects. If it is not to be a mere empty form, it must be directed to some human interest as its object.

From this point of view the right of an individual over his own personality is in essence a right directed towards an abstract interest. Every person has a right to his life, to his honour and good repute, to freedom of action, of speech, of conscience. The corresponding duties lie, firstly, on the world at large, that is, on all members of a society, as well as of other societies which are at peace with it; secondly, the subject of the corresponding duty may be the society or commonwealth itself, in so far as it may be prevented by public law from curtailing the life, liberty, or reputation of its subjects.

In so far as objects of rights may be regarded as possessing marketable value they are called " property." Not every object of right admits of such an estimate; a person's honour or reputation, for instance, cannot be appraised either for consumption or for sale, although heavy damages may be awarded for a wanton or malicious attack on it.   On the other hand not only concrete things like estates, houses, furniture, but also abstract interests, such as the goodwill of a firm or the copyright of a novel, have a value in the market and therefore form items of property in the special sense of the word.

A term peculiar to English law is *chose in action :* it means the right of a person to recover from another by legal proceedings any money or property. The "thing" in this case is the material interest involved in the success of the action.

CHAPTER IV

FACTS AND ACTS IN LAW

1. A NETWORK of legal rules stretches over social life, the events of which are constantly crossed by the lines of juridical rights and obligations : most circumstances of any importance assume a certain legal aspect. Thus as against the various facts and acts of business, intellectual intercourse and social relations, rises a series of facts- and acts-in-law on which depend the changes and evolution of rights. It is hardly necessary to point out that these juridical facts and acts do not simply reflect their counterparts in ordinary life : they have special attributes of their own, as the layman is often made to feel.

Let us begin with an examination of facts-in-law. The word *fact* as opposed to *law* is sometimes used by lawyers of circumstances which have a bearing on the decision of a legal problem. The production and sifting of evidence has to deal with facts in this sense. In so far every minute peculiarity of

a thing, of a person or of a process may prove
of value, *e.g.* footprints or fingerprints may
be of the greatest importance in identifying
a criminal.   On the other hand it is clear that
a detective or a counsel collecting evidence to
establish guilt will do well not to drag in
circumstances which have no importance for
the prosecution and which would merely
confuse the problem in hand.   Indeed, the
judge may object in the course of an examination of witnesses to irrelevant questions and
to the bringing in of unnecessary material.
In this case, however, although certain legal
forms make themselves felt, the aim of the
process is the settlement of a question of
fact as opposed to a question of law—has a
murder been committed or not ? or is it a
case of manslaughter ? or of a brawl which
led to the infliction of a fatal wound ? has
this particular man, the prisoner, committed
the crime ? did he do it of his own motion
or at the instigation of another ? In so far,
the examination turns on matters of ordinary
social experience : and therefore the decision
of all such questions is commonly left to a
jury composed of laymen, for whom the
questions at issue have to be put clearly and
carefully by the Court.   But suppose these

questions have been answered in one way or another : suppose the jury has brought in the verdict that A was slain in a quarrel by a companion who was drunk at the time. As soon as this has been established, we have to deal with facts-in-law. The fact of accidental death in consequence of an unpremeditated assault, and the fact that the slayer was intoxicated, lead to legal consequences : a sentence will be pronounced by the Court, which will formulate these consequences in the particular case according to certain legal rules provided with a sanction. As far as the judicial decision is concerned, the whole story of the quarrel, with its minute incidents and details, will have faded away, leaving the verdict as its one result. In this verdict the rule and rights set in operation by the Court will still depend on facts : but these will be " facts-in-law," the mere skeleton, as it were, of the event itself, from which all irrelevant circumstances have been removed. The slayer may have been a rather sympathetic, though hot-headed person, the slain obnoxious and contemptible; but these features will disappear from the fact-in-law as irrelevant : for the law cannot draw such distinctions, and the right of a worthless person to be protected in life and limb is as sacred as the right of the noblest of citizens. Just as the fact appears in a kind of schematic outline, so does the person slain become a man in general, a man in law, if one may use the expression, bereft of all attributes except the one essential quality of being possessed of a full right to have his life protected by the State. Again, intoxication may become an important fact from the point of view of law. It will not be relevant to point out that the wine consumed was bad in quality or that the criminal was apt to be irritable and violent when drunk. The judges, while taking the fact into consideration as an important condition in the settlement of legal consequences, will fix their attention strictly on one feature of intoxication—the one relevant feature from the legal point of view, that is, the effect of liquor on the mind of the criminal and the consequent increase or decrease of responsibility.

To sum up, we must recognize two entirely different kinds of facts, which indeed exist not only in juridical theory, but in actual technical distinctions of law. Thus in the law of evidence there are on the one side the " facts which prove "—the materials which help to establish the " fact in issue " : and on the other side, the " facts which are to be proved "—those things which as soon as they have been established by evidence, become definite facts-in-law.

A curious example of the kind of legal problems which arise in this connection may be given from an American case, the *State of Iowa* v. *Bell* (1870). A man was found at night hiding in a room of a neighbour's house, to which he had obtained access by stealth. It would have been a clear case of attempted burglary if the evidence had not shown, fortunately for the accused, that he was drunk at the time. The inference suggested by the judge and accepted by the jury was, that the prisoner did not realize at the time that he had betaken himself to a strange house. It would, however, be very unsafe to rely on intoxication as a mitigating circumstance in an English or American Court in a case of murder or manslaughter. Far from that, it has been repeatedly laid down by judges that the fact of intoxication need not entitle a criminal to lenient treatment.

Similar questions as to fact would arise in estimating the amount of moral pressure exerted on a person making a will or a contract, or in ascertaining the degree of care or negligence shown by a person to whose keeping somebody else's goods have been entrusted. Sometimes the Court will have to probe very deep into social and moral conceptions of the time, or of a certain social environment, in order to disentangle the facts-in-law on which legal consequences of rights and duties depend. In any case a process of sifting evidence from real life is necessary in order to obtain even a comparatively small number of facts-in-law.

2. We must also notice that law sometimes has to build up its pronouncements as to rights and duties on the strength not of real, though select facts, but of presumptions of facts as they appear in the aspect officially recognized by law. The old doctrine of evidence was prolific in artificial rules in this respect. Bentham used to inveigh violently against the phantoms produced by this artificial treatment of evidence and the travesty of right which was often produced by it. His philippics were not in vain, and a great many simplifications and improvements have been achieved since his time. Even now, however, our law is not entirely free from artificial rules which may sometimes

endanger the dispensing of strict justice. My readers will doubtless remember the case of the murderer Crippen. A specially damning piece of evidence against the accused consisted in the finding of a portion of his pyjamas under the floor of the house with the remains of the body of his victim. Now this piece of evidence had not been produced originally by the prosecution, and it was employed only by way of rebutting certain allegations made by the accused. Its introduction at the eleventh hour supplied Crippen's counsel with a ground for trying to have the verdict quashed in the Court of Criminal Appeal.[1] " Rebutting evidence," it was pleaded, " which could have been given in chief as part of the case for the prosecution, cannot be given to strengthen the case for the prosecution after the evidence on both sides has been closed."

The reason for these restrictions is not difficult to see; the intention of the law is that the prosecution shall not be able to keep back material arguments till the last stages of the trial in order to produce them at unexpected moments, when counsel for the accused is not prepared to meet them. But it is clear that the rigid application of the rule

[1] *R. v. Crippen* (1910).

might have had deplorable effects in Crippen's case, inasmuch as it might have removed from the consideration of the jury the question as to the year when the pyjamas were made, which was very material to the issue. Fortunately the Court was able to exercise its discretion in the matter. But there are many cases in which evidence very valuable in substance has to be ruled out on formal grounds.

Besides these rules of evidence, Courts are sometimes bound to accept certain well-established legal *presumptions* and artificial facts-in-law instead of real and ascertainable facts. It is an accepted rule, for instance, that children born in wedlock are presumed to be the legitimate offspring of the father, even if it should be possible to prove that the mother at the time of conception actually cohabited with another person. The rule is intended to prevent anybody attempting, except on indisputable evidence, to raise the intricate questions connected with illegitimacy; but it is clear at the same time that it may often lead to the suppression of truth. The Courts have to be content in this matter with presumed instead of actual facts. In this way, the legal rules, although they usually serve some clearly reasonable purpose, may in some instances obscure the real truth of the case under consideration. But this is perhaps inevitable : for law is framed to suit average conditions and may fail to disentangle exceptional circumstances.

3. Here, as in many other cases, it is evident that the methods of law aim only at approximations : and since this is so, there are many important elements which cannot receive explicit treatment by the Courts. For instance, it is often difficult to satisfy by legal means our natural craving for moral retribution : and not infrequently the way in which law approaches problems of individual responsibility seems inadequate from the point of view of moral feelings. This insufficiency of method, however, is the result not of callousness on the part of tribunals, but of the fact that it is impossible to probe psychological situations by the means of strict legal standards. Take, for instance, the treatment of seduction in English law. The strict theory is that if a girl over sixteen has been seduced, damages are recoverable from her seducer only for the actual loss of services sustained by her parent or master. At the same time, it is often evident that in assessing damages a jury will be actuated by

its reprobation of the defendant's conduct;
and this attitude is not discouraged by
judges. It was once observed by Lord
Chancellor Eldon :

"Although in point of form the action
[for seduction] only purports to give a
recompense for loss of service, we cannot
shut our eyes to the fact that it is an action
brought by a parent for an injury to her
child, and the jury may take into their
consideration all that she may feel from the
nature of the loss. They may look upon
her as a parent losing the comfort as well
as the service of her daughter, in whose
virtue she can feel no consolation; and as
the parent of other children whose morals
may be corrupted by her example."[1]

It is clear that the method of strict law is
inadequate to embrace all the real elements of
the case, and it might be urged that perhaps
a more stringent treatment is necessary for the
seduction itself : but it is easy to see what
difficulties would arise if the law attempted
to apply exact methods to such questions.

4. The expression *fact* is sometimes extended in English legal usage to all questions

[1] *Bedford* v. *McKowl* (1800).

examined and decided by Courts without reference to established rules of law. It may happen that there is no rule bearing directly on points raised in a trial : the Court has, however, to take a definite stand as to the problem. Such matters are sometimes termed points of fact, although by their consideration in the given case a basis of law would be established and they would then pass from the domain of fact into that of law.

Thus in cases where the terms of a statute are in dispute and no authoritative decision as to their interpretation has yet been given, a Court will interpret the terms in accordance with the facts of the particular case, and will give a decision as to those facts, which on subsequent occasions will be appealed to as a matter of law. In a recent case [*Dallimore* v. *Williams* (1912)] the plaintiff engaged certain musicians to perform at a concert for a fixed rate of remuneration; the defendants, who were officials of the Amalgamated Musicians' Union, objected to the rate of pay, and by means of circulars, picketing and threats, induced some of the musicians to break their contract with the plaintiff. Now to induce a breach of contract by such means is, under ordinary circumstances, a wrong for which

a

damages may be recovered : but by the Trade
Disputes Act, 1906, a *trade union* inducing a
breach of contract *in furtherance of a trade
dispute* is exempt from liability. The question therefore was whether in this case the
dispute was technically a " trade dispute " :
if so, the officials of the union could not be
made liable. At the trial, the judge directed
the jury that a " trade dispute " was one either
between an employer and his employees, or
among employees themselves. A verdict was
returned for the plaintiff, from which the
defendants appealed. The Court of Appeal
held that too narrow an interpretation had
been placed upon the term " trade dispute "
by the judge in the court below, and that it
might be made to cover a dispute between an
employer and a trade union, such as existed
in the present case.[1] In so deciding, the Court
expressly stated that its decision was not
governed by any definite authority as to the
interpretation of the term, for the principal
case relied on by the plaintiff [*Conway* v.
Wade (1909)] was held to have been decided
on other grounds, and therefore not to be

[1] A new trial was ordered: at the second trial the
plaintiff was awarded £350 damages. See *The Times,*
June 18th–20th, 1913.

binding in the present instance. Thus the Court was really deciding a question of *fact*, which, however, in all future cases where the same point arises will, on the strength of this decision, be treated as a question of *law*.

But I am bound to say that this peculiar use of the term " fact " is subject to criticism from a jurisprudential standpoint. It may be inconvenient to speak of law where there is no legal rule to meet the case, but it is still less appropriate to speak of fact where the point at issue does not touch either the circumstances of the trial or the material conditions on which the application of a rule depends. One might class such instances as matters for judicial decision or interpretation, or for legal consideration and decision. From a wider point of view they would certainly belong to law in so far as they affect the aggregate of principles on which social order depends.

5. It has been made clear by the above remarks that the principal importance of establishing facts-in-law consists in supplying necessary links between the circumstances and events of ordinary life and the rules of law. In order to manifest legal rules in concrete cases, the exact points at which the

rules apply have to be ascertained, and it is
in these points that facts-in-law are located.
They have a double aspect: they are ex-
tracted from reality, and they serve as conditions for the application of rules and the
creation or modification of rights and duties.
Let us take one or two instances. I pick up
a shell by the seashore; my doing so is a
fact-in-law: it creates for me a right of
property in the shell, and sets in motion the
rule that a thing not belonging to any particular individual belongs to the first person
who appropriates it. Should a passer-by
snatch the shell from my hand, a second fact-
in-law would arise: it would be a delict
against property on his part and he would
become the subject of a duty to restore the
shell or its worth to me, possibly to pay a
fine for the infringement of order, while I
should have an action and a claim of right
against him in tort. Or again, A is the owner
of a house, of some furniture, of money at
the bank. He dies without leaving a will.
His death is a fact-in-law which calls into
operation the rules as to intestate succession.
His solicitor advertises for heirs. A distant
cousin appears and asserts his right to the
inheritance. Besides the fact-in-law—*i.e.* the

death of A—which has opened the succession, the claimant would have to produce other facts-in-law, a certified pedigree, eventually witnesses to establish his own descent, perhaps the death or legal disappearance of other relations, and so forth. It might be said that among the innumerable facts of actual life some become accentuated as links in the formation, modification, or assertion of rights. These are facts-in-law.

6. Another group of legal counterparts to events of real life consists of " *acts-in-law.*" An act-in-law is necessarily personal because it requires a subject. Its essence is the exercise of a will. It also requires an object, because the act of a person is always directed towards some definite aim. Such objects vary widely, but they have one attribute in common : they are all varieties of right. The proposition expressing an act of law may be stated in the following typical manner : I (subject), create, modify, abolish, or transfer (predicate), a right (object). The difference from an ordinary act is evident. Ordinary acts admit of all kinds of predicates, with or without juridical consequences (*e.g.* I eat a cake, I write a letter, I write a book), while the predicates in sentences expressing acts of

law take the shape either of the constitution, abolition, transfer, or modification *of a right*. Therefore the sentence " I ride my bicycle " does not refer to an act-in-law, although it undoubtedly refers to the exercise of a right. But the sentence " I give my bicycle to you " does refer to an act-in-law, namely, to the transfer of my right to another person. Lastly, there is a difference as to objects, since the objects of acts-in-law are rights, while the objects of ordinary acts are as multifarious as the realities of the material or the spiritual world.

An act-in-law is similar to an act of legislation. The latter is effected by society, the former by members of society; the latter creates and abolishes rules, the former creates and abolishes rights—in so far, of course, as an individual member is allowed by society to create and to abolish rights. In a sense it may be said that representatives of society itself, such as judges or administrative officers, may act in law when their action or direction consists in the concrete attribution of rights. A judgment conferring on the plaintiff a right of possession which has been wrongly exercised by the defendant may be said to constitute an act-in-law. The action of justices of the peace, conferring a licence on the owner of a public-house, is an act-in-law. In another sense crimes and torts are acts-in-law in so far as they produce legal consequences and create rights and duties as to compensation. But in the first case the judges and officers act as mouthpieces of the State, though it may not always be easy to distinguish between the elements of law-making on the one hand and of government and the attribution of rights on the other; in fact, the latter is derived from the former. In the second case the principle of the action creating rights is exactly the reverse of that which is embodied in acts of law conforming to substantive rules. The subject creates legal consequences against his will; it is the reaction from his intended act which constitutes rights. Therefore both administrative acts and delicts had better be kept by themselves as distinct groups of actions constituting rights.

The technical term " act-in-law," which is more familiar to Continental than to English lawyers in its equivalent forms, *negotium, Rechtsgeschäft, acte juridique,* applies primarily to actions of individual citizens intentionally constituting or modifying rights. We should perhaps mention here the subdivision of acts-in-law into two classes, *unilateral* and *bilateral.*

A testament or donation may serve as an example of a unilateral act : here it is only the intention of one person—the testator or the donor—which is material (although the act is complicated by the requirement of acceptance on the part of the devisee or donee). Bilateral acts-in-law require the consensus of two or more wills, as may be seen in the familiar cases of sale, lease, or bailment.

7. When I speak of the intentional constitution or modification of rights, I do not mean that the subject of the act-in-law is bound to realize clearly and fully the legal consequences of his action. Very often laymen effect acts-in-law without a clear knowledge of their legal consequences. Thus an undergraduate hires furnished rooms for the academic term : he knows, of course, that he is making an agreement which binds him to pay rent and not to damage the furniture, while the landlady is obliged to let him stay in the rooms for, some eight weeks. But I doubt whether the ordinary undergraduate realizes when he makes the agreement how far an unexpected event, say a contagious illness in the house, would relieve him from his obligations, or to what extent the landlady

has a right of entering the rooms against his will or a right of ejectment if rent be in arrear, and the like.   I presume that even students reading law would find it hard to answer all questions as to the possible legal consequences of this contract.   Yet the undergraduate who takes lodgings undoubtedly effects an act-in-law.   His general purpose is directed towards the creation of rights and obligations, and therefore his resolve to take the rooms is construed as an act-in-law with all its premeditated and unpremeditated legal consequences.   In the same way in ordering a suit from a tailor a person acts in law, although he may not be aware of the precise legal rules which govern the transaction. Similarly a person may suppose himself unable to perform certain acts-in-law, and yet may be held by a Court to have performed them and to be legally responsible for them. Thus in *Chapple* v. *Cooper* (1844), Mr. Cooper's widow was sued by an undertaker for the expenses of her husband's funeral.   She was under age at the time of her husband's death, and therefore pleaded that she was not bound by the contract, since she was an infant at the time it was made.   Now it is a rule of law that while an infant is generally unable to make valid contracts, he may do so for *necessaries* and for things which are clearly for his benefit. The question therefore was whether the burial of a spouse was a " necessary " within the meaning of the rule. The Court held that it was both " a personal advantage, and reasonably necessary." Now it is clear that Mrs. Cooper certainly did not realize the legal consequences of her act when she arranged with the undertaker, but that did not prevent the Court from drawing inferences from her contract and holding her bound by it.

8. What is needed, therefore, is a general intention to constitute or to acquire rights, to constitute or to assume obligations. In the simplified psychology of legal doctrine intention is ascribed to the will as such and called the element of free will.

In order to ascertain whether a person really meant to exert his will by an act-in-law, one of two methods may be followed. In ancient times an act-in-law had to be clothed with elaborate forms which were not only intended to serve as proof of the transaction, but also helped to show that the subject of the act had had the deliberate intention of performing it. Under feudal law, a person making a grant of land was obliged to go through a ceremony of investiture of which the surrender of a flag, stick, sod, or the like formed the principal part. Disputes might often arise as to whether the ceremony had been precisely followed, and a valid conveyance effected. In course of time the formalities were simplified and made subservient to the general intention. The motives which led to the transitions are well shown in a seventeenth-century case,[1] in which it was said that, " although most properly livery of seisin (*i.e.* formal conveyance) is made by delivery of a twig or turf of the land itself, whereof livery of seisin is to be given; and so it is good to be observed; yet a delivery of a turf or twig growing upon other land; of a piece of gold or silver, or other thing upon the land in the name of seisin is sufficient, and when the feoffor is upon the land, his words without any act are sufficient to make livery of seisin; as if he saith, ' I deliver seisin of this land to you in the name of all the land contained in this deed '; or such other words, without any ceremony or act done." Even at the present day, however, certain survivals keep up the memory of old forms : thus when

[1] *Thoroughgood's Case* (1612), as reported by Coke.

a person making a lease places his finger on a wafer representing a seal, and pronounces the sacramental words, " I deliver this as my act and deed," he is performing an act suggested by the long history of formal conveyance.

But modern jurisprudence is generally averse from such formalism, which it considers not so much a guarantee of certainty as a possible trap for the unwary. The existence of a free will generating the act-in-law is usually ascertained by direct investigation, which may be difficult to carry out, but which satisfies the more developed sense of justice better than mere form. A signed document would still be required in important cases, e. g. for the purpose of conveying land, but precautions are taken that such documents should not be obtained by intimidations or fraud. A party may plead in rescission of a formally correct sale that he was made to sign the deed under duress, or that a draft which had been prepared and signed for future delivery subject to certain conditions had been surreptitiously appropriated by the other party. Or again, a party to a contract may maintain and bring evidence to prove that the agreement was entered into on the strength of fraudulent misrepresentations.

Here, as in many other cases, the law has only very imperfect means of determining the element of free resolve in the subjects of acts-in-law. Too often presumption takes the place of conviction established by cogent proof. But this drawback is rather due to the legal treatment of typical transactions than to any special failing of the theory of acts-in-law. It is exceedingly difficult to take hold of intentions by the help, as it were, of legal pincers, and we have to be content in law with approximations. The law sets up a standard of reasonable conduct, which ought to fit the requirements of average persons. It assumes that in certain given circumstances a reasonable man will normally act in a certain way. For example, it assumes that when a man makes the promise of a benefit to another, he generally does so in consideration of some benefit to himself : therefore it is a rule of English law that in any agreement not embodied in a formal deed under seal, there must be some " valuable consideration," that is, an actual benefit to the promisee, or an actual detriment to the promisor : and if a man makes a purely gratuitous and informal promise, he may in law repudiate it at any moment, though he may be under the strongest *moral* obligation to redeem it. At one time it was held by Lord Mansfield that a moral obligation would constitute sufficient consideration in law : but this view never met with general acceptance, and in modern theory consideration must have some actual material value. Thus in *Thomas* v. *Thomas* (1842) a promise by a person to grant a cottage to the widow of his brother deceased was held not to be supported by the " moral consideration " of pious respect for the wishes of the deceased : but inasmuch as the widow had promised a rent of £1 and the expense of repairs, that was held to be sufficient " valuable consideration " to make the agreement binding.

Very difficult problems arise from the fact that obligations are sometimes entered into on the strength of misrepresentations. The Court has to decide how far the person induced by such misrepresentations to perform an act-in-law has been deprived of the exercise of his free will. Very often it is not easy to make a distinction between an error of judgment, which the Courts are not called on to rectify, and a misconception induced by fraud, which from the point of view of law entitles the person deceived to a remedy. I will give one case in illustration of the difficulties of the position, and the means by which a Court may solve them.

In *Redgrave* v. *Hurd* (1881) R., a solicitor, advertised that he had a moderate practice with extensive connections and was shortly retiring, and would take as partner an efficient lawyer who would not object to purchase R.'s suburban residence, valued at £1600. H. answered and asked for an interview, at which R. said the practice brought in an income of about £300. H., after a rather careless inspection of the books, thought that the practice might be worth not £300 as was stated by R., but about £200; and thereupon signed an agreement to purchase the house, without having a reference to the practice inserted in the agreement. He entered into possession, and finding that in fact the practice was worthless, refused to complete the purchase of the house. R. then brought action to compel him to do so. H. resisted on the ground of misrepresentation as to the value of the practice, and the Court decided in his favour. One of the grounds of decision was stated by Sir George Jessel in the following terms :

" If a man is induced to enter into a contract by a false representation, it is not a sufficient answer to him to say that if he had used due diligence, he could have found out that the statement was not true.

" One of the most familiar instances is where men issue a prospectus in which they make false statements of the contracts entered into before the formation of a company, and then say that the contracts themselves may be inspected at the solicitor's offices. It has always been held that those who accepted those false statements as true are not debarred from their remedy because they neglected to look at the contracts."

9. Besides the analysis of the act-in-law as an expression of free will, it has to be examined from the point of view of its conformity with accepted rules. Of course, an individual citizen or an association cannot aspire to the power of creating rights or dealing with rights in a way forbidden by the law of the State to which they belong. Their activity in producing rights is necessarily subordinated to the legal framework established by the commonwealth. It would be idle, for instance, to bequeath money to a church, say

to the Roman Catholic Cathedral in London, for the purpose of saying Masses for the soul of the testator. Such an act-in-law, which would be perfectly valid in Spain or in Italy, would be void in England by a Statute of 1547, which forbids "superstitious practices."

The necessity for the act-in-law to conform with received rules goes further : it is admitted that acts in law which clash with received notions of morality or public policy are legally void. The institution of a prize for the purpose of remunerating the most artful deceit performed within the last year would not be upheld by any tribunal, although it might be unimpeachable in form and the cases of deceit admitted for competition might keep clear of criminal prosecution. It has been held that a bequest made on the condition that a person should not enter the army or navy is void at law because the condition is clearly against public policy [*In re Beard: Beard* v. *Hall* (1908)].

In a recent case which has attracted some attention through its quaint setting, a theatrical manager had entered into a contract with a theatrical agent to arrange a certain sensational incident for the purpose of advertisement. Two ladies, engaged by

H

the agent, entered the stalls in extravagantly large hats which they refused to remove, whereupon they were ejected by the manager. Subsequently they took proceedings for assault, but the magistrate found that the manager was within his right in removing them from the theatre. When Mr. Dann, the agent, claimed the fee agreed upon for arranging this interlude and fictitious trial, the theatre manager, Mr. Curzon, refused to pay, and the Court had to decide whether the act-in-law was of such a nature as to be binding on the parties. It was held that it was not. The judges thought that the simulated offence and purpose of advertisement for which it was enacted showed a disrespect for the function of justice and were in so far directed against public utility. Therefore in spite of the clear consent of the parties in formulating their agreement this act-in-law was declared void [*Dann* v. *Curzon* (1910)].

In these cases, the contracts were contrary to " public policy." But the law goes even further, and refuses to uphold any contract which is based on *private* immorality. On the principle " *Ex turpi causa non oritur actio,*" it refuses to recognize the validity of any contract the purpose of which is clearly immoral. Thus in a recent case [*Upfill* v. *Wright* (1911)] the defendant was sued for the rent of a flat in Southampton Row. It was shown in evidence that the plaintiff's agent, at the time when he executed the lease, knew that the defendant was the mistress of a certain man who visited her constantly at the flat. The Court therefore found that the plaintiff, through his agent, deliberately let the premises for an immoral purpose, and that he was unable to recover the rent. The principle is clearly stated by Mr. Justice Bucknill : " If a woman takes a house in order to live in it as the mistress of a man and to use it for that purpose, and the land-lord at the time when the lease is executed knows that it is taken for that purpose, the landlord cannot recover the rent."

CHAPTER V

1. TURNING now to a special consideration of rules of law, we have to ask from what sources they are derived. The expression " sources " may be used in different ways. We may talk of Bracton's treatise or of the Year Book as sources of English mediæval law, meaning that we derive a considerable part of our knowledge of English mediæval law from them. Similarly students of history speak of the sources for the history of Elizabeth's reign, meaning the various contemporary narratives and documents. But we are not now using the word " source " in such a general sense. We are inquiring by what processes rules of law may be evolved, and whether these processes point to certain kinds of authority as the sources from which such rules are technically derived. It is not difficult to see that in spite of all the variety of legal systems in force in different countries

and at different ages, legal rules emanate from a certain limited number of authoritative sources, and that in the process of their elaboration they follow certain grooves according to the character of their origin.

To begin with, it seems clear that a law may be either *made* in advance for the express purpose of regulating future events, or else *declared* by Courts of Justice in the exercise of their jurisdiction. Herein is the fundamental distinction between *legislation* and *judge-made law*.

An Act of the Parliament of Great Britain may serve as an example of a law enacted by legislators. Codification aiming at the reduction of separate and discrepant laws to one system appears merely as one of the modes of legislation, *e.g.* the Code Napoléon in France, or the new Civil Code (*Bürgerliches Gesetzbuch*) in Germany.

As for judge-made law, it may assume one of three aspects :

(1) *Customary law*, which comprises legal rules based on traditional usage and declared in popular courts : the customs observed in the borough courts of Southampton or of Nottingham,

for instance, or the custom of gavel-kind succession in Kent.

(2) *Judicial decisions* form the basis of rules evolved by judges, and serve in their aggregate as material for the case law of which the English and Anglo-American common law are such conspicuous instances.

(3) *Equity* in its jurisprudential sense is derived from the discretion of judges or arbitrators in applying general considerations of justice and fairness to the decision of legal conflicts.

The *law of nature* or of reason has been regarded by some, but by no means by all jurists, as a set of rules dictated to man by nature itself and therefore obligatory for all commonwealths.

The sources mentioned may be examined in different order in accordance with the main purpose which the student has in view. I will take them in the order of my enumeration not because it is the order corresponding to the probable historical sequence in which they arose, but because it is the most convenient, as it seems to me, for the purpose of exposition, since it proceeds from simpler to more complex forms of law-making.

2. An Act of Parliament, or statute, aims emphatically at the formulation of legal rules in a definite manner. English Acts commonly use side by side expressions which have the same or nearly the same meaning, in order to prevent attempts at evading a law on the pretence that some particular term of phraseology does not occur in it. Observe, for example, the abundance of synonym in the following passage (Gaming Act, 1845, s. 17) :

" Every person who shall, by any fraud, or unlawful device, or ill-practice in playing at or with cards, dice, tables, or other game, or in bearing a part in the stakes, wagers, or adventures, or in betting on the sides or hands of them that do play, or in wagering on the event of any game, sport, pastime, exercise, win from any other person to himself or any other or others, any sum of money or valuable thing, shall be deemed guilty of obtaining such money or valuable thing from such other person by a false pretence, with intent to cheat or defraud such person of the same, and, being

convicted thereof, shall be punished accordingly."

If there be a written constitution which
requires a special process for modification or
amplification, laws made by legislative bodies
are subject to revision from the point of
view of their conformity to this constitution.[1]
A notable example is seen in the legal system
of the United States, where the Supreme Court
has power to determine the " constitution-
ality " of laws passed by Congress and ratified
by the President, as well as those passed by
different States of the Union. Thus in 1801
a certain Marbury was appointed by the
President to the Office of Justice of the Peace
in the district of Columbia. The appointment was confirmed by the Senate, and a
commission made out, signed and sealed,
but not transmitted to Marbury. At the
last moment, circumstances came to light
which made the appointment undesirable,
and Madison, the then Secretary of State, refused to deliver the commission. Marbury,
however, contended that his title was complete, since the office was not subject to

[1] In this case the constitution appears as a fundamental
law to which all other laws have to be subordinated.

removal by the President; he therefore applied to the Supreme Court, under s. 13 of the Judiciary Act, 1789, for a writ of mandamus, which is an order to compel the executive officer to act in accordance with the legal claim. The application was refused on the ground stated by Chief Justice Marshall : " That the provision of the Judiciary Act purporting to give the Supreme Court juris- diction, in a proceeding original and not appellate, to issue writs of mandamus to public officers was not warranted by the Constitution, and was therefore inoperative and void " [*Marbury* v. *Madison* (1803)].

3. It is clear that when a competent legis- lature has made a law in accordance with the Constitution, the Courts cannot overrule it and are bound to give effect to it. It would be wrong, however, to suppose that statutes, however carefully formulated, reduce the application of the law to a mere mechanical process of bringing a given case under a given section. It is plain that however explicit the words of a statute may be, a Court must determine the exact meaning of the phrase- ology before it can apply the law. Attempts have sometimes been made to get rid of this necessity of judicial interpretation : for

example, the introduction to the Prussian Code of 1794 went so far as to forbid all interpretation as distinct from direct application, and ordered that tribunals should lay all cases of doubtful verbal meaning before a special committee of jurists and statesmen.[1] This device, however, proved entirely unsuccessful, for it was found impossible to draw a precise line between application and interpretation, and to reduce a Court to the functions of a mere sorting-machine. Statute law or codified law necessarily consists of sentences, the words of which may be differently understood by different people; and the first duty of a Court is therefore one of *literal interpretation*. The law-reports abound with examples of this necessity, which is perpetually imposed upon tribunals, and which often gives rise to difficult problems. Let us take an example from one of the Workmen's Compensation cases, which have been so numerous of recent years and have raised so many points of literal interpretation. In *Nisbet* v. *Rayne and Burn* (1910) the facts were that one Nisbet had been employed as a cashier by the defendants, a firm of coal-

---

[1] Secs. 47 and 48 of Introduction to the Prussian *Landrecht*, repealed in 1798.

owners : and it was part of his duties to take
every week from the office to the colliery the
cash out of which the wages of the employees
at the colliery were paid. While so engaged,
he was robbed and murdered. Now under the
Workmen's Compensation Act, 1906 (s. 1),
when a workman has met his death by an
accident " arising out of, and in the course
of his employment," his widow may claim
compensation from the employers. Nisbet's
widow claimed under the section : but one
of the questions in the case was whether a
murder could be considered an " accident "
within the meaning of the Act. It was contended for the defendants that " accident "
essentially implies the absence of intention;
whereas a murder is clearly a deliberate and
intentional act on the part of the criminal.
But the Court held otherwise. Lord Justice
Farwell said :

" The intention of the murderer is im-
material : so far as any intention on the
part of the victim is concerned, his death
was accidental; and although it is true
that one would not in ordinary parlance
say, for example, that Desdemona died by
accident, this is because the horror of the

crime dominates the imagination and compels the expression of the situation in terms relating to the crime and the criminal alone; it would be quite natural to say that a man who died from the bite of a dog or the derailment of a train caused by malicious persons putting an obstacle on the line, died by accident."

And Lord Justice Kennedy said :

" An historian who described the end of Rizzio by saying that he met with a fatal accident in Holyrood Palace would fairly, I suppose, be charged with a misleading statement of fact. . . . But whilst the description of death by murderous violence as an ' accident ' cannot honestly be said to accord with the common understanding of the word, wherein is implied a negation of wilfulness and intention, I conceive it to be my duty rather to stretch the meaning of the word from the narrower to the wider sense of which it is inherently and etymologically capable, that is, ' any unforeseen and untoward event producing personal harm,' than to exclude from the operation of this section a class of injury which it is

quite unreasonable to suppose that the
Legislature did not intend to include within
it."

Sometimes the interpretation of a term
may be complicated by the fact that a word
has changed in meaning since the enactment
of the statute in which it is employed. An
example of this change or extension in the
meaning of a word is provided by a recent
case [*Pollard* v. *Turner* (1912)], in which the
appellant had employed a boy to deliver
bread, which was carried from door to door
in a basket affixed to a bicycle. The Bread
Act, 1836, enacts that any person who carries
bread for delivery in a " cart or carriage "
shall be provided with scales and weights
with which the bread may be weighed on
demand by any purchaser. The boy did not
carry scales and weights, and his master was
charged under the Act. The question was
whether a bicycle could be considered a
" cart or carriage " within the meaning of
an Act which was passed before bicycles were
known. The Court of Appeal held that it
might be so considered, and the conviction
was affirmed.

Sometimes the respect of judges for the

actual words of a statute may be so great that they will consider themselves bound by the exact phraseology, even though the effect of so doing may be to produce awkward consequences in the law. This principle of literal interpretation is well illustrated by a recent trade union case which has attracted considerable attention [*Vacher* v. *London Society of Compositors* (1912)]. An action of libel and conspiracy to publish libels was brought by plaintiffs, a company of printers, against defendants, who were the trade union of compositors. There is a provision in the Trade Disputes Act, 1906 (s. 4, subsec. 1) to this effect : " An action against a trade union . . . in respect of any tortious act alleged to have been committed by or on behalf of the trade union shall not be entertained by any court." Libel and conspiracy to publish libels are, of course, torts at common law ; the defendants did not dispute the torts, but claimed immunity under the section cited. Now in all other sections of the Act in which immunity for wrongful acts is given, the wrongful acts are specified as being done " in contemplation or furtherance of a trade dispute " : and it was argued that, although these words were not contained in s. 4, sub-sec. 1, the Legislature meant them to be understood : for this, it was said, was an inference to be drawn from the construction of the whole enactment. The Court of Appeal, however (Lord Justice Farwell dissenting), refused to read the words into the section, and held the defendants exempt. The effect of this judgment is, to quote Lord Justice Farwell, practically to give trade unions " a licence to commit torts (in plain English, to injure their neighbours) with impunity, and to inflict losses and misery on all or any of his Majesty's subjects as long as they please, without responsibility " : and it was argued that the Legislature could not have intended anything which was so clearly contrary to public policy; but Lord Justice Kennedy said : " I decline to speculate in regard to any statutory enactment which it becomes my duty to interpret as to what was the policy to which the Legislature thought it was giving the effect of the law." The House of Lords upheld the decision of the majority of the Court of Appeal, and expressly approved the judgment of Lord Justice Kennedy. The Lord Chancellor (Viscount Haldane) said that he did not propose to speculate concerning the motive of Parliament.

The topic was one on which judges could not profitably or properly enter. Their province was the very different one of construing the language in which the legislature had finally expressed its conclusions, and if they were to undertake the other province, they were in danger of going astray in a labyrinth to the character of which they had no sufficient guide.

4. Another group of problems arises in connection with what may be called *technical interpretation*. Very often a statute is concerned not merely with general principles of social order which are more or less intelligible to everybody, but with the regulation of some highly technical matter which requires special knowledge. In these cases, the Court has not merely to determine the general meaning of a word, but the peculiar technical significance which the Legislature intended to convey.

Such technical points may arise in cases which at first sight seem quite straightforward. In *Unwin* v. *Hanson* (1891) the plaintiff claimed damages for the cutting and mutilation of certain trees. Under the Highways Act, 1835, if a man's trees are growing so as to exclude light and air from the highway he may be ordered to " prune or lop " them :

and if he fail to do so, the surveyor of highways, on the authority of two Justices of the
Peace, may enter and " prune or lop " the
trees. An order under this Act was issued
against the plaintiff, and, as he failed to
comply with it, the defendant (surveyor of
highways) entered, and, among other things,
cut the tops off two fir trees. The plaintiff
claimed that he had no statutory power to do
this. Evidence was given at the trial to show
that the term " lop " is used in agriculture
and forestry of cutting off branches laterally,
while the technical term for cutting off the tops
of trees is to " top." The Court therefore held
that the surveyor had exceeded his statutory
powers. " If the Act," said Lord Esher,
" is one passed with reference to a particular trade, business, or transaction, and
words are used which everybody conversant
with that trade, business or transaction, knows
and understands to have a particular meaning
in it, then the words are to be construed as
having that particular meaning, though it
may differ from the common or ordinary
meaning of the words. For instance, the
' waist ' or ' skin ' are well-known terms as
applied to a ship, and nobody would think
of their meaning the waist or skin of a person

I

when they are used in an Act of Parliament dealing with ships."

It is not to be expected that judges will be experts in all the multifarious technical matters with which statute law deals : and therefore they have often to look for the explanation of a term or a precept to technical information supplied by specialists. Unfortunately, however, it happens only too often that experts will give conflicting opinions or vague indications which it is not easy to put into juristic shape. Take the following clause of the German Civil Code : [1] " A person may lose the power of disposing of his property, if he cannot attend to his business affairs on account of mental disease or mental debility." What is mental disease and what mental debility from the scientific point of view ? What abnormal conditions of the mind justify a court in decreeing that a person should be put under curatorship or forbidden to dispose of his property ? How are limits to be drawn between states of health justifying complete and partial loss of the power of disposition ? Medical science will supply lay inquirers with rather vague and contradictory answers to these questions.

[1] S. 6, 1. Cf. s. 104, 3 and s. 114.

It will probably tell them that the relation between mental disease and mental debility is not easy to discover from the medical point of view, and that it would be quite out of the question to connect the full loss of dispositive power with disease and the partial loss of it with mental debility. It is not easy to utilize such advice for the purpose of deciding a case. The Court will have to fall back on common sense or legal tradition in most instances of this kind. I should like to give one example of the perplexing problems which are sometimes set to judges and juries. Though the case I am about to cite deals with the construction of a common law rule and not of a statutory clause, it will sufficiently illustrate the problems of interpretation to which I refer. In *Regina* v. *Burton* (1863), the prisoner, a youth of eighteen, was indicted for the murder of a boy. It appeared that the deceased boy had been playing on the Lines, a public place at Chatham, where the prisoner saw him, and was seen near him. Some hours afterwards, the child's dead body was found on the Lines. The throat was cut, and there were marks of a violent struggle. The police were engaged in prosecuting their inquiries, when the prisoner gave himself up, and admitted the act, recounting all the circumstances with perfect intelligence. He added: "I knew the boy, and knew his mother, but I had no particular ill-feeling against the boy; only I had made up my mind to murder somebody." A doctor deposed that the prisoner's mother had twice been to a lunatic asylum and his brother was of weak intellect. . . . The witness had attended the prisoner himself on two occasions, and believed he was labouring under what, in the profession, would be considered as "moral insanity," that is, he knew perfectly well what he was doing but had no control over himself.

Mr. Justice Wightman, in summing up the case, said that as there was no doubt about the act, the only question was whether the prisoner, at the time he committed it, was in such a state of mind as not to be responsible for it. In *M'Naughten's Case* (1843), the judges laid down the rule to be that there must, to raise the defence, be a defect of reason from disease of the mind, so as that *the person did not know the nature and quality of the act he committed, or did not know whether it was right or wrong.* Now to apply this rule to the present case would be the duty of the jury. It was not mere eccentricity of conduct which made a man legally irresponsible for his acts. The medical man called for the defence defined homicidal mania to be a propensity to kill; and described moral insanity as a state of mind under which a man, perfectly aware that it was wrong to do so, killed another under an uncontrollable impulse. This would appear to be a most dangerous doctrine and fatal to the interests of society and to security of life. The question was whether such a theory was in accordance with law. The rule laid down by the judges was quite inconsistent with such a view; for it was that a man was responsible for his actions if he knew the difference between right and wrong.

The jury, on this interpretation of the law, found the prisoner guilty, and he was executed.

The case illustrates an important principle of technical interpretation : it will be seen that although expert opinion was given in the case, it was subject to searching judicial review. Thus, even in matters of the most technical nature, the ultimate opinion must rest with the Court.

5. Sometimes the best way to ascertain the meaning of a clause will be to consider the

actual elaboration of the enactment. Minutes of committees' debates in Parliament, drafts of documents and of examinations of witnesses, may enable us to revive, as it were, the state of mind and the process of reasoning in legislators or negotiators of treaties. French Jurisprudence especially has made great use of this method of *historical interpretation* in construing Napoleon's Code in the sense in which its clauses were drafted in the Conseil d'État in 1804.

An interesting example of the same method has recently been before the public in this country. When a Bill was introduced in the Congress of the United States of America for the regulation of traffic through the Panama Canal, and it became apparent that a discrimination as to rates would be made between ships belonging to the United States and those of other countries, Great Britain entered a protest against such discrimination on the ground that it infringed Clause 111 of the Hay-Pauncefote Treaty of 1901. The clause reads :

" Art. III, 1 : The canal shall be free and open to the vessels of commerce and of war of all nations observing these rules, on terms of entire equality, so that there shall be no discrimination against any such nation, or its citizens or subjects, in respect of the conditions or charges of traffic, or otherwise. Such conditions and charges of traffic shall be just and equitable."

On the side of the United States it was contended that the clause forbids discrimination not between all Powers without exception, but between all Powers using the canal with the exception of the United States, who are building the canal and will administer it when completed. Should we limit our consideration of the clause to its actual words, the question would hardly admit of a conclusive solution. Each side might support its .interpretation by plausible arguments : but, as was urged by European jurists, the matter assumes a different aspect if one recalls the circumstances and negotiations which led up to the Hay-Pauncefote Treaty. Firstly, it was always assumed that the administration of the canal would be organized on the lines of the Declaration of Constantinople, which regulated the use of the Suez Canal : and in that document no preference was given in regard to rates to any Power. Secondly, it was pointed out that the Hay-Pauncefote Treaty was substituted for the Clayton-Bulwer Treaty of 1850, which contained among other provisions a clause [1] which was thus interpreted by Mr. Blaine (Secretary of State under Cleveland) in a dispatch to Lowell (United States Ambassador at the Court of St. James): " The United States did not seek any exclusive or narrow commercial privileges. It agrees, and will proclaim, that the same rights and privileges, the same tolls and obligations, for the use of the canal shall apply with absolute impartiality to the merchant marine of every nation of the globe."

It is not our purpose here to consider the merits of the rival contentions in this case, but it is probable that if it ever came before the Hague Tribunal, the method of historical interpretation of the disputed clause would not be disregarded.

The method is evidently quite appropriate in order to discover the intentions of lawgivers or negotiators of treaties. But it has never been much in favour in the practice of English Courts ; and even on the Continent it is recognized more and more that circumstances may have changed so much since the time

[1] Art. VIIL

of the original promulgation that it would be preposterous to bind the Courts strictly to the views which obtained at that time.

6. A very important group is formed by the interpretation of clauses in which the words and terms are not difficult to understand, but the rule itself is so general and vague, or so antiquated, that the Court has to add limitations or subdivisions of its own to supply gaps or to modernize the application of the rule.   In such cases the interpretation is not merely literal, but may be called *widening interpretation.* In its capacity of interpreter the Court is, strictly speaking, precluded from introducing new principles and from modifying or correcting the existing law : but, as we have seen in connection with literal interpretation, a court cannot be limited to mere mechanical functions, and this is especially so when judges are called on to determine not merely the exact significance of a particular term, but the general aim and effect of a statutory provision.   Here it is often necessary for Courts to interpret clauses by somewhat complicated methods, and not infrequently the effect of this wider interpretation is to supply gaps in existing laws. An instance is furnished by the Statute of

Frauds, which in its fourth section provides that

> "No action shall be brought whereby to charge . . . any person . . . upon any contract or sale of lands tenements or hereditaments or any interest in or concerning them, or upon any agreement that is not to be performed within the space of one year from the making thereof unless the agreement upon which such action shall be brought or some memorandum or note thereof shall be in writing and signed by the party to be charged therewith or some other person thereunto by him lawfully authorized."

But on the fringe of the clause, as it were, there remained several doubtful points which have required much judicial interpretation : for example, the important question whether the course of the year mentioned in the clause is to be reckoned for both parties or only for the defendant : and thus it has been necessary for the omissions in a single section of this Act to be filled up by a long and laborious process of judicial interpretation—which, indeed, is even now far from complete.

An interesting instance of interpretation which supplies, as it were, the place of a provision missing from a statute, is to be found in the judgment of the Privy Council in a Canadian case [*The Attorneys-General of the Provinces of Ontario and others* v. *The Attorney-General for Canada* (1912)]. The point raised was whether or not an Act of the Dominion Parliament authorizing the putting of questions either of law or of fact to the Supreme Court and requiring the judges of that Court to answer them on the request of the Governor in Council, was a valid enactment within the powers of that Parliament. It was argued by the Provinces that "no Legislature in Canada has the right to pass an Act for asking such questions at all." The power to ask questions of the Supreme Court, sought to be bestowed upon the Dominion Government by the Act impugned, was so wide in its terms as to admit of a gross interference with the judicial character of that Court, and was therefore of grave prejudice to the rights of the Provinces and of individual citizens. Any question, whether of law or fact, it was urged, could be put to the Supreme Court, and they would be required to answer it *with their reasons.* Though no immediate effect was to result from the answer so given, and no right or property was thereby to be adjudged, yet the indirect result of such a proceeding might and would be most fatal. When the opinion of the highest Court of Appeal for all Canada had once been given upon matters both of law and of fact, it was said, it was not in human nature to expect that, if the same matter were again raised upon a concrete case by an individual litigant before the same Court, its members could divest themselves of their pre-conceived opinions; and thus there might ensue not merely a distrust of their freedom from prepossession, but actual injustice, inasmuch as they would in fact, however unintentionally, be biassed.

The Judicial Committee, however, decided against these contentions, and gave the following reasons, among others, for their decision :

" In the interpretation of a completely self-governing Constitution founded upon a written organic instrument, such as the British North America Act, if the text is explicit the text is conclusive, alike in what it directs and what it forbids. When the

text is ambiguous . . . recourse must be had
to the context and scheme of the Act. Again,
if the text says nothing expressly, then it is
not to be presumed that the Constitution
withholds the power altogether. On the
contrary, it is to be taken for granted that
the power is bestowed in some quarter, unless it be extraneous to the statute itself (as,
for example, a power to make laws for some
part of his Majesty's Dominions outside of
Canada) or otherwise is clearly repugnant to
its sense. . . .

" Is it then to be said that a power to
place upon the Supreme Court the duty of
answering questions of law or fact when put
by the Governor in Council does not reside
in the Parliament of Canada ? This particular power is not mentioned in the British
North America Act, either explicitly or in
ambiguous terms. In the 91st section, the
Dominion Parliament is invested with the
duty of making laws for the peace, order,
and good government of Canada, subject to
expressed reservations. In the 101st section,
the Dominion is enabled to establish a
Supreme Court of Appeal from the Provinces.
And so when the Supreme Court was established it had and has jurisdiction to hear

appeals from the Provincial Courts. But of any power to ask the Court for its opinion, there is no word in the Act. All depends upon whether such a power is repugnant to that Act."

The Judicial Committee came to the conclusion that it was not repugnant. They observed that the right of putting questions to the law courts as to the state of the law had been exerted and was still extant under the Constitution of Great Britain, that the Dominion Parliament had made use of this right six times without its actions being challenged, and that the Provinces actually exercised that right in regard to their own Courts. Under these circumstances, the Judicial Committee thought that there was no juridical ground for declaring the Act passed by the Dominion Parliament to be invalid.

Striking instances of widening interpretation are afforded by the problems set to the ingenuity of the judges of the Supreme Court of the United States by the necessity of subordinating the expansion of modern civilization to the provisions of a constitution framed in 1788. Any attempt on the part

of legislators to make laws excessively rigid
must inevitably compel tribunals to put as
wide a construction as possible on their
power of interpretation : and this result has
undoubtedly been produced by the obstacles
which the Constitution of the United States
has opposed to its own amendment.[1]

Article I, s. 8, of the Constitution of the
United States contains a number of clauses
conferring on the Federal Legislature the
power to make laws for the Union in regard
to certain specified matters. One of the sub-
sections of s. 8 empowers Congress to coin
money and to regulate its value, while another
confers upon it the power to regulate commerce with foreign countries and between
different States. Both sub-sections gave rise
to contradictory interpretation. Under s. 8
Congress declared the paper notes issued by
the United States legal tender for the payment of debts, in spite of the fact that the

[1] As is well known, an amendment can only be *initiated*
by a majority of two-thirds of both Houses of Congress,
or two-thirds of the legislatures of individual states ; it
can only be *carried* with the consent of a majority of
three-fourths of the legislatures or of the Constitutional
Conventions. These provisions make the process of
amendment practically unworkable—except by political
convulsions like that of the Civil War. which led to the
passing of Articles 13, 14 and 15.

paper money brought a much lower price in the market than the gold and silver coins to which its units nominally correspond. When the Legal Tender Law was enacted in 1870, private individuals refused to accept notes at their face value in payment for debts, and when the cases came up for decision, the Supreme Court began by giving a strict interpretation to the clause of the Constitution and invalidated the law passed by Congress as unconstitutional, because there was no mention in the clause of a power to give notes an artificial value as against coined money. In consequence of changes in the composition of the Supreme Court, however, this interpretation was overruled as early as 1871, and the Legal Tender Law was admitted to be within the power conferred by clause 8.

Another difficulty arises under this clause with regard to the regulation of commerce. The power of Congress to regulate interstate commerce implies, of course, that commerce within each State is to be regulated by the authorities of the State. Yet the interdependence of the various departments of commerce is very great, and it was found impossible to assign jurisdiction strictly according to territorial divisions. As one of

the judges of the Supreme Court (Justice
Moody) put it: " It is said that Congress has
never before enacted legislation of this nature
for the government of interstate commerce
by land. . . . The fundamental fallacy of
this argument is that it misunderstands the
nature of the Constitution . . . and forgets
that its unchanging provisions are adaptable
to the infinite variety of the changing conditions of our national life. . . . It is not
too much to say that the large needs of the
factory and the household are no longer dependent on the resources of the locality, but
are largely supplied by the products of other
states." As regards the transport of goods,
it was held that the Federal Government had
authority even when certain parts of the
transport service were in the hands of carriers
within the limits of a particular State. In
the case of the *Daniel Ball,* a steamer plying
within the State of Michigan, the Supreme
Court stated the doctrine for the first time:

" If the authority of the United States
Government does not extend to an agency
in such commerce when that agency is
confined within the limits of a State, its
entire authority may be defeated. Several

K

agencies combining, each taking up the commodity transported at the boundary line at one end of a state, and leaving it at the boundary line at the other end, the federal jurisdiction would be entirely ousted, and the constitutional provision would become a dead letter."

The principle was naturally extended to transport by land. On the other hand, the Supreme Court has insisted hitherto on drawing a line of delimitation between commerce and manufacturing industry, treating the first as an interstate concern even when a particular firm of merchants is established in some single State, but refusing to extend the same view to factories. In 1906 Congress passed a law providing " that every carrier engaged in such commerce should be liable to any of its employees for all damages caused by the negligence of any of its officers, and that the fact that the employee was guilty of contributory negligence should not of itself bar recovery "; but the Supreme Court declared this Act of Congress to be unconstitutional, because it " applied in terms to any of the employees of a firm and thus affected employees not engaged in interstate and foreign commerce." It is very difficult, however, to uphold strictly this line of cleavage, and the Supreme Court will probably be constrained to widen its interpretation of the clause.

7. As a result of all these observations we are entitled to say, I think, that legislation as a source of law is inseparable from a process of interpretation by the Courts, which in itself amounts to a subordinate source of law. It is impossible to curtail the freedom of judges in analysing cases and applying general rules in ways not indicated in the rule and not premeditated by the legislators. Thus in the simplest and most emphatic expression of the law-making power of societies, we find that another factor asserts itself by the side of that of deliberate prospective commands, namely, the force of public opinion and of professional opinion as manifested in the action of judges. They are undoubtedly persons in authority, but their voice has a decisive weight in such questions not merely on account of this external authority, but chiefly by reason of the necessities imposed by logic, by moral and by practical considerations.

CHAPTER VI

1. CUSTOM as a source of law comprises legal rules which have neither been promulgated by legislators nor formulated by professionally trained judges, but arise from popular opinion and are sanctioned by long usage. The word " custom " may mean a great deal besides this; it may, for instance, denote the usual behaviour of men in certain circumstances; thus in the inquiry into the *Titanic* disaster, attempts were made to ascertain whether or not it was customary for captains of ships to reduce speed when near icebergs. The apportionment of responsibility for torts and crime, as well as the interpretation of contracts, often turns on the consideration of such habits and presumptions. But these inquiries into habitual behaviour have nothing to do with what is termed *customary law* or *legal customs*. The latter is restricted to rules regulating rights when those rules are established not by legislators or by professional

lawyers, but by popular practice. Primitive law is to a large extent based on such customs, while with the progress of society they tend to be displaced by express legislation and by rules elaborated by lawyers. The historical school led by Savigny attached the greatest importance to this source of law : it was in their view the unsophisticated sense of the nation in regard to questions of right. Being based on national character and on the opinions of the people, custom was regarded by them as the outward expression of latent principles which were sure to be more in keeping with the notions of justice ingrained in a given society than the artificial creations of statecraft or of scientific jurisprudence. They pointed out how such artificial super-structures were often doomed to destruction on account of the latent hostility with which they were received by the people for whom they had been built up: how powerless purely rationalistic contrivances are apt to be when brought in contact with realities governed by entirely different psychological tendencies : and they contended that the surest method for rearing a durable and imposing edifice of positive law was to build it up on foundations supplied by national custom and historical usage. But the enthusiasm for this particular source of law has cooled down a great deal, and the teaching of the historical school has been subjected to most searching and hostile criticism.

Laws and legal customs are undoubtedly coloured by historical circumstances, and depend to a great extent on the complex result which may be described as national character or national spirit. Germans treat questions of law and right in a very different way from Frenchmen or Englishmen. But they also write poetry and paint pictures in a different way, and yet no one would think of defining poetry or painting as the expression of national ideas in literature or art. We are asking what law, literature, art mean, and not how they are affected by national character.

The leaders of the historical school always spoke of legal custom as the creation of a people at large : while in reality most customs arise from local usage, and legal customs like those of mediæval Germany or mediæval France present a bewildering variety of provincial, municipal, manorial and professional rules : and it is only by State legislation and by the centralizing work of Royal Courts that national unity is gradually evolved. A striking example of the growth of custom and its incorporation into the common law is provided in England by the Law Merchant. Originally the rules governing mercantile intercourse grew up by usage, and were recognized among merchants themselves as possessing binding authority. These customs in England were throughout a long period a definite body of special rules administered by local courts with the help of professional experts : but in course of time, and under the influence of great lawyers like Lord Mansfield, they became absorbed into the common law. This body of particular customary law is, as was said in a well-known case, " neither more nor less than the usages of merchants and traders . . . ratified by the decisions of courts of law, which, upon such usages being proved before them, have adopted them as settled law " :[1] and at the present day most of the rules are to be found embodied in the Sale of Goods Act, 1893.

The mystic talk about popular conviction as to law originates to a great extent in a confusion between opinion and positive rules, while at the same time special wisdom

[1] *Goodwin* v. *Robarts* (1875).

is often assumed in cases in which it would have been equally wise to go either to the right or to the left, and custom merely testifies to a moré or less casual choice between two or three equally expedient courses. Why should two witnesses be required to make a will and not three, or why should it be necessary to summon a party three times before claiming the intervention of an official to help to bring the recalcitrant opponent to trial? As a matter of abstract wisdom, two or four times would do equally well.

Lastly, if popular custom is natural and characteristic in early stages of legal history, as a child-like speech and manners are natural and characteristic of infancy, it would be as preposterous to try to fetter advanced civilization by rudimentary customs as it would be to dress a grown-up man in a child's clothes. A stage is necessarily reached by any progressive community when naïve and traditional notions of right must give way before sharper dialectics and systematized learning. The fact that law becomes more and more the special province of professional lawyers is neither strange nor regrettable.

2. In spite of these criticisms, perfectly justified in themselves, there is a core of sound

reason in the study of custom as one of the
sources of law. Even highly developed
systems do not pretend to fix every particular
of legal arrangements by central agencies,
but leave a considerable margin in the adjustment of local interests not only for bye-laws,
but also for traditional customs. Readers of
Mr. Eden Phillpotts' interesting novel, *The
Portreeve*, will remember the description of the
antique customs of the Duchy of Cornwall
which govern pastoral pursuits on Dartmoor.
Moor-men who possess Venville Rights are
entitled to depasture their beasts on the
common of the Moor; and in order to insure
that these rights are not arrogated by " foreigners," the curious ceremony of the colt-
drift is performed. The appointed day for
the drift is kept a secret, so that the " foreigners " may be taken unawares and fined for
their presumption; and when the time comes,
all the ponies on the common are " rounded
up " into the pound, and there marked for
future identification. The ceremony is the
more interesting because it probably goes
back to practices even more ancient than the
feudal period—in any case unconnected with
manorial arrangements. A great deal, too,
of the law of copyhold is based simply on

manorial custom : although under the Copyhold Act, 1894, this form of tenure is subject
to compulsory enfranchisement, and there is
consequently a tendency for it to disappear,
yet so long as it continues in existence, there
are many points connected with individual
estates which are referable only to the " custom of the manor " : and thus the usages of
a feudal society are often of the highest
importance to the rights of individuals in the
twentieth century.

3. It must not be supposed that custom is
a valid source of English law merely because
it has in fact been recognized and acted upon.
Before it can become part of the law of the
land it has first to pass certain judicial tests.
Thus before a custom can have validity in
law it must be shown to be both *certain* and
continuous : and besides these elementary
requirements, it must have an *existence from
immemorial time.* The period of " legal
memory " is supposed in English law to run
from the accession of Richard I (1189); but
in practice, it is not necessary to prove the
continuous existence of custom from that
time. The legal requirements in this respect
are well summarized by Cockburn, C.J., in
Dalton v. *Angus* (1881). In that case the

question at issue concerned what is legally termed the " right of lateral support." The general rule of law is that a man is entitled to lateral support for his land—*i. e.* if A and B are adjoining landowners, A cannot excavate his own land in such a way as to undermine B's. But this right of support does not in general extend to buildings upon the land; and the question in this case was whether the right might be acquired for buildings by *prescription*.

The Chief Justice, dealing with the history of the limitations of the legal prescriptive period, used certain expressions which apply generally to the judicial interpretation of " legal memory." Having mentioned that the Statute of Westminster (1275), as applied by the Courts, fixed the limit of the period at the accession of Richard I, he continued :

" As might have been foreseen, as time went on, the limitation thus fixed became attended with the inconvenience arising from the impossibility of carrying back the proof of possession or enjoyment to a period, which, after a generation or two, ceased to be within the reach of evidence. But here again, the legislature not intervening, the judges provided a remedy by holding that if the proof was carried back *as far as living memory would go*, it should be *presumed* that the right claimed had existed from time of legal memory, that is to say, from the time of Richard I."

Again, in modern English Courts custom must pass the test of *reasonableness*: that is it must be reasonable in its application to the circumstances of individual cases. It does not follow, however, that because a custom in one particular locality runs counter to a general rule of common law, it will therefore be held to be unreasonable. In *Wigglesworth* v. *Dallison* (1778) the plaintiff was a leaseholder and the defendant his landlord. After the plaintiff's lease had expired, the defendant entered upon the land and took away the growing crop : whereupon the leaseholder brought an action of trespass. The defendant relied on the contention that the land was his property in freehold, and that after the lease had expired he had a right to resume possession and take the growing crop, since it was a general rule of law that a tenant could not claim a crop which was sown by him before the determination of his lease, and which he knew would be ripe for cutting after the lease had expired. The plaintiff, however, set up as against this general rule a local custom that the tenant should take the " way-going " crop. The Court found this custom proved, and Lord Mansfield said : " We have thought of this case, and we are all of opinion that the custom is good. It is just, for he who sows ought to reap, and it is for the benefit and encouragement of agriculture. It is, indeed, against the general rule of law concerning emblements (*i. e.* growing crops), which are not allowed to tenants who know when their term is to cease, because it is held to be their fault or folly to have sown, when they knew their interest would expire before they could reap. But the custom of a particular place may rectify what otherwise would be imprudence or folly."

On the other hand, a custom which can be shown to be of great antiquity will sometimes be repudiated by the Courts if its rigid application to modern circumstances would be so harsh and inconvenient that it would be unreasonable to enforce it. This point is suggested by the fact that, in spite of all their reverence for ancient usages and forms, English Courts find it necessary not to yield to custom on purely formal grounds. Things of immemorial growth may be tainted by very backward conceptions of right and of public duty. In *Mertens* v. *Hill* (1901), Mertens sued, as lord of the manor and soke of Rothley, which had belonged to King Edward the Confessor and William the Conqueror, to recover from defendant a customary fine of one shilling in the pound in respect of a piece of land recently conveyed to him, and alleged to be within the ambit of the manor and soke. Rolls of courts in the possession of the lord of the manor, and dating from 1575, were produced. A manorial custom in a manor of ancient demesne to exact a fine on alienation to a foreigner was held bad, under the Statute *Quia Emptores* (1290) and on other grounds, as being a restriction on the right of a freeman to alienate. The Court was clearly led to its decision by the view that it would be unreasonable and unjust to keep up the antiquated customs which prevailed for centuries in manors of ancient demesne in respect of the alienation of land. For modern lawyers, such rates and fines as were inflicted on the freeholders of the soke of Rothley were absurd, and it is in this conflict of the modern principle of free trade with feudal customs that the real reason for the decision must be sought. The appeal to the Statute *Quia Emptores* was, in fact, a historical misapprehension; this enactment was never meant to regulate the sale of land within such an estate as the soke of Rothley, and as a matter of fact fines on alienation were levied in different ways for many centuries after the statute had been passed. But the objection to the custom, though it may have been bad from a historical point of view, was a weighty one from the point of view of modern legal and economic principles.

4. But it is clear that if custom has once been legally recognized, it cannot be judged by modern standards alone. To some extent ancient standards will have to be recognized even in modern surroundings : and it will sometimes happen that although a custom has quite lost its original significance, it will still be upheld in modern times. Certain customs connected with land-tenures may have been amply justified by feudal conditions, but will be quite incongruous in a modern civilization : yet they may be enforced by the Courts. Copyhold tenure affords a curious example in the custom of *heriot*. In mediæval

times it was usual for a lord to provide the outfit for his tenant; for military followers, this outfit would be war-equipment, part of which fell back to the lord as a heriot at the death of the tenant. For peasants, the equipment would be agricultural, and a similar heriot was exacted in the shape of the *best beast* (or best chattel). On copyhold lands similar customs are recognized even in modern times. In itself the custom of heriot certainly cannot be justified by reasonable considerations nowadays : indeed, as long ago as 1709 it was declared by a Lord Chancellor [1] to be, from the point of view of *equity*, " unreasonable, the loss a family sustains thereby being aggravated " : and yet customs of heriot are often upheld at the present time, chiefly on copyhold tenements. Thus in *Harrison* v. *Powell* (1894) the defendant was lord of a manor, and on the death of a certain tenant, entered on the land, which was in occupation of the deceased's executors, and marked two horses and a cow : and later on, again entered, took away the beasts, and sold them. The executors claimed damages for trespass and for seizure of the cattle. The records of the manor were carefully examined; the Court

[1] *Wirty* v. *Pemberton.*

came to the conclusion that a heriot custom was proved, and that the defendant was therefore perfectly entitled to enter and take the beasts.

English Courts have not only to consider the operation of ancient customs in modern conditions, but also to understand, and often to respect, the customs of other civilizations. It would be the grossest travesty of justice if English judges, in considering the custom of (say) India or Burmah, were guided solely by European conceptions of right and wrong. The jurisprudence of the Judicial Committee of the Privy Council affords many signal instances of a respectful treatment of foreign popular customs.

In a case of 1906—*Musammat Lali* v. *Murli Dhar*—the question at issue was one of disputed succession. The respondent claimed the property not only as the adopted son of the deceased, but under a will contained in a *wajib-ul-arz.* This word means literally " that which it is necessary to record or state." It is really a " record of rights," which, besides registering the rights of individuals in various proprietary or possessory relations, records many village customs—*e. g.* in regard to market-tolls, local usages connected with land-

L

tenure—in fact, all matters relating to village administration. It was highly important in the case that the Court should consider the nature and effect of the document, and it was admitted that as a record of purely customary institutions, the *wajib-ul-arz* was legal evidence which an English Court was bound to consider. The peculiarity in such cases is that European lawyers have to make an effort to assume a point of view which is foreign to their own minds, but which has directed the thought of the native parties. For example, in a case before the Privy Council in 1906—*Kannepalli Suryanarayana* v. *Pucha Venkataramana*—a husband had authorized his wife to adopt to him a son. Twenty-four years after her husband's death, she adopted a boy, but the child died a few months afterwards. Thirteen years later she adopted another son. The question was whether this second adoption was valid. Clearly it was contrary to the most elementary English legal and social ideas; but the two objects of the deceased husband—" to secure spiritual benefit to himself and to continue his line "—were held " meritorious in the view of Hindu law," and therefore deserving of recognition by an English Court.

5. In order to study the operation of custom

in all its significance and bearings, it is best
to turn to earlier periods of legal history. By
observing the peculiarities of the process of
law-making during these earlier periods we
obtain clues which may be found valuable
even in regard to later developments. The
first thing to be noticed is that legal customs
often arise independently of any litigation,
by the growth of definite views as to rights
and duties. Familial authority was regulated
chiefly by such views as were adapted to
economic requirements and social conditions.
Monogamy, polygamy, polyandry, group
marriage, began as usages of daily life before
they took shape as legal customs. So did
marital authority, emancipation, succession
to goods and succession to land. The history
of intestate succession is rich in examples of
interesting changes in the formulation of rules,
and all these changes were originally produced
by the operation of non-litigious custom.
Whether all the children had to share in the
succession of the father, or whether sons
inherited land to the exclusion of daughters,
or whether the eldest or the youngest came to
the hearth and landed estate: these and similar rules were certainly not commands of
authority, nor rules primarily evolved in the

course of trials, but practical arrangements
of the interested persons, approved by the
opinion of their neighbours and gradually
ripening into customary rules which could be
appealed to in case of litigation.   The fact is
worth notice, because the rules in question are
by no means unimportant and certainly
cannot be accounted for on the Austinian
theory of State command.   In the same way
the English law of real property grew up with
constant reference to important rules created
by the usage of the country-side, *e.g.* rules as to
cultivation of open fields, the use of meadows
and pastures, the delimitation of boundaries,
and so forth.   Or take the law of persons, and
notice the growth of rules as to serfdom and
gentle birth.

It is impossible to construe customary law
purely on the principle of instinctive or
conscious repetition of the same rules, as some
jurists have attempted to do, or to explain it
by prescription, as the doctors of Canon Law
were fond of doing; both elements contribute
greatly to uphold customary rules once they
are formed, but they cannot account for their
origin and growth. Mechanical repetition
may serve to explain the formation of usages—
e. g. rights of way—but how does it apply in

the case of fundamental legal institutions like marriage, succession, contract, etc. ? Obviously it does not : and we are thus driven to assume, in spite of the obscurity with which such early institutions are necessarily surrounded, that there was a conscious activity of elders, priests, judges, witans, or experts of some kind directed towards the discovery and declaration of what is right and just : a process of discovery which, however mystically imagined and solemnly presented, must really have consisted in the formulation of rules as emergency required in accordance with popular conceptions of right. Fortunately we are not left without direct evidence as to this process of discovery and declaration. It is expressly described in Germanic legal history as the " finding and manifestation of law " (*das Recht finden, das Recht weisen*). The assessors of a Frankish tribunal had to " find the law " for parties who had challenged them by a solemn formula (*tangano*) to do so. The *Schöffen* of mediæval German law had to formulate decisions (*Urtheile*) at every step of a trial, in order to solve the string of questions of law and fact which were put to them. The *lagmen* of Scandinavian courts, who at a later period were not unknown in

the Danish districts of England, also held the
position of judicial authorities declaring the
law. What their functions were in this
respect may be gathered from the fact that
the ancient provincial laws of Sweden consisted of pronouncements by these authorities.
This institution assumed a most peculiar shape
in Iceland, where we find a kind of judicial
professor (*loegsoegumadhr*) who delivered before the general assembly consecutive courses
of instruction on the law to be applied in
Iceland.

In Saxon England the wise-men (*witan*) in
the county courts and in the central assembly
of the kingdoms held similar functions, and
later on the mediæval Parliament came to
be considered as the chief organ for the
declaration of law.

6. One consequence of the organic character
of this process of law-making is shown in the
fact that it may still be resorted to in our own
times if there arises the problem of regenerat-
ing a given system by appeal to national
traditions and popular ideas, as opposed to
foreign influence and artificial enactments.
A striking instance of this kind is presented
by German law, which for centuries was
flooded by the conceptions of a professional

jurisprudence reared on Roman law and rely-
ing on Justinian's *Corpus Juris* as the principal
source of legal rules. The revival of Germanistic jurisprudence which we have witnessed
within the last fifty years is connected with
an ardent study of legal antiquities and of
customary law. This remarkable process
found expression in the writings of numerous
lawyers and historians of the law who formed
the group of so-called Germanists. It reacted
also on the compilation of the new German
Code. The first draft of this Statute book
was elaborated by a commission composed
chiefly of jurists brought up on Roman law :
but when this draft was published, it called
forth the violent opposition and criticisms of
the Germanistic school. Consequently, it had
to be recast, and in its present shape it affords
a curious compromise between conflicting
tendencies. It would be impossible to review
the numerous and important peculiarities
imported into it by the study of German legal
history and custom, but I should like to point
out a few instances in which the influence of
Germanistic ideas is especially conspicuous.
The doctrine of ownership is conceived in a
much less absolute and abstract manner than
in the sources of Roman Law; the more

concrete view of property right is derived 'to a great extent from the historical notion of Germanistic possession (*Gewere*), which may be briefly characterized as a presumption of title, in contrast with the sharp opposition between property and possession obtaining in Roman Law. Again, the doctrine of corporations, instead of starting from the fiction of unity, is developed on the basis of a dualism between the life of the union and of its component members. As regards the acquisition of property, the chief stress is laid on " good faith," and property once acquired in good faith is protected even against the claim of a rightful owner. Such are a few of the features of Germanistic legal theory, which may be paralleled by many others.

In fine, we may say that customary law appears as the judge-made law of periods when the judges are still intimately connected with the people they represent, and feel bound to declare popular legal lore rather than to supply links in a system of learning.

CHAPTER VII

1. THE force of judicial opinion, which asserts itself clearly in the working of promulgated law and of custom, acts as an independent source of law when there is no legislation bearing on particular points which arise in practice. In countries where codified and enacted law prevails, such points will occur on account of the gaps left by statutes and the clauses of a code. But there are countries in which statutes cover only part of the ground, while most of the current litigation is met by decisions of the Courts based on the considered opinion of judges. I need not remind my readers that Anglo-American common law is pre-eminently judge-made law. Such law may also be called case-law, because it is formulated not in general prospective enactments, but in pronouncements called forth by particular cases. This process of formulation involves several characteristic consequences.

169

To begin with, no sharp distinction can be drawn between customary and common law. The latter is historically the ordinary and customary law of the kingdom, while the domain of custom proper is more or less restricted to the practice of local and popular Courts. Gavelkind succession—*i.e.* equal division of inheritance in land among sons— was the custom of Kent and of some other localities, while primogeniture and the taking of inheritance by daughters as joint co-heirs was reputed to be the common law of England as regards military tenures. This latter custom, however, only became part of the common law because it had been declared and approved by the Courts of the kingdom : no one could have said when and by whom it had been established in the first instance. It was deemed to be derived from customary practice as to fiefs and sergeanties; it had been used more or less in all the feudal Courts : but its actual formulation as a rule of law was the work of the King's judges. In this way many of the fundamental principles of common law may be traced to mediæval custom.

But if in this way legal origins were sometimes hidden in the twilight of feudal and Anglo-Saxon institutions, in other instances common law principles were asserted spontaneously on important occasions by the Bench of a High Court on the strength of general notions of justice or of some doctrine suggested perhaps by foreign learning. For example : originally there was no action to protect a leaseholder against ejectment by his landlord : but about 1235 the King's Bench, on the initiative of William Raleigh, began to entertain actions brought by tenants for a term of years against landowners who had ejected them before the completion of their term. Bracton, in his famous treatise on the Laws of England, was quite right in comparing this new departure of judge-made law with the great reform of Henry II's which provided the freeholder with remedies against dispossession. It is evident that Raleigh's doctrine was not prompted by precedent, but suggested by the necessities of justice and possibly by the study of Civil Law.

The beginnings of common law have necessarily to be traced to those pronouncements in which the opinion of judges was as yet unfettered by the weight of previous decisions, and the Year Books show conclusively that in the early stages of legal evolution principles of law were declared and developed with a great deal of independence, and there were many contradictions in the views expressed by leading judges on different occasions. In the fifteenth century, for instance, the authorities of the Bench wavered for a long time before they settled once for all that if a person promise to perform certain acts, and if the promise is made in view of a benefit to himself, or involves a loss to the promisee, then he is liable to damages not only if he performs them badly, but also if he fails altogether to perform them.

Gradually, however, the search for precedents assumes great importance. In the absence of a statute, a Court before whom a dispute is tried informs itself whether similar cases have been decided before, and if so, how the decision has gone. If exactly similar cases have occurred before, the judges in subsequent cases have an easy task. They usually appeal to the former decision and frame their own on its pattern. In some instances they are even obliged to do so. In England, in particular, a certain hierarchy of the Courts makes it impossible for a lower Court to deviate from the course indicated by a decision of a superior Court. A County Court is bound to accept as law a decision of the

High Court; the High Court is bound to follow decisions of the Court of Appeal, and the Court of Appeal cannot overrule a decision of the House of Lords, which is the highest judicial authority in the kingdom : and the House of Lords cannot overrule its own decisions. When Courts stand on the same level, or when the precedent has to be drawn from the jurisdiction of an inferior Court, such precedents are not absolutely binding, though they are generally treated with respect.

Circumstances may arise in which it is necessary to restrict or even overrule a previous decision. The following case provides an example, and serves to show how decisively the judgment of an authoritative Court will sometimes be overruled. In *Rex* v. *Russell*, the defendant, in order to facilitate his business, had erected some staiths in the river Tyne, and the question in the case was whether they were an impediment to navigation. Mr. Justice Bayley, in charging the jury, took the view that the erection did not merely give a private advantage to the defendant in the way of his business, but was a *public benefit*, inasmuch as it was a means of bringing coals to market at a lower price and in better condition than would otherwise have been possible : and this so-called public benefit would, in the opinion of the learned judge, countervail any slight public inconvenience which might arise from the presence of the obstruction in the river. This view was afterwards upheld by a Court consisting of the trial judge (Mr. Justice Bayley), Mr. Justice Holroyd, and Lord Chief Justice Tenterden. In 1873 similar circumstances arose in *Attorney-General* v. *Terry*, where the defendant enclosed part of the river Stour, and proposed to erect a scaffolding which, it was contended, would be a public obstruction to navigation. Counsel for the defendant relied on *Rex* v. *Russell*, admitting that a slight obstruction would be created, but urging that this was counterbalanced by the " public benefit " to trade. The Court, however, refused to follow the previous case. Sir George Jessel, Master of the Rolls, held that in such cases " the public " must be considered not as the public at large, but as the public (*i. e.* the majority of individuals) *of a particular place :* and it was too remote a benefit to say that the encouragement of a single individual's trade was a benefit to "the public." With regard to *Rex* v. *Russell*, he made this emphatic statement : " Now I must say that *Rex* v. *Russell* in my opinion is not law, and it is right to say so in the clearest terms, because it is not well that cases should continue to be cited which have been virtually overruled, although judges have not said so in express terms."

It sometimes happens that, for somewhat inscrutable reasons, a more or less irrational doctrine will be set up by a superior Court, and will continue to be binding authority on inferior Courts until some tribunal of high standing definitely pronounces against it. One of the most interesting examples of this kind is the so-called " Doctrine of Identification." It used to be held that if a man were travelling in some conveyance, and an accident occurred through the negligence of another, and the passenger was injured thereby : and if the person controlling the conveyance in which the passenger was travelling had been guilty of contributory negligence: then the passenger must be considered as so far " identified " with the driver that he could not claim damages against the other negligent person. The leading authority for this doctrine was *Thorogood* v. *Bryan*, decided in 1849. In that case, a claim was made by a widow under Lord Campbell's Act : her husband had been travelling in an omnibus, and when stepping off it had been knocked down and killed by another omnibus. It was shown that both drivers were at fault : and the widow's claim was refused on the ground stated by Mr. Justice Maule, that "the deceased must be considered as identified with the driver of the omnibus in which he voluntarily became a passenger, and the negligence of the driver was the negligence of the deceased." It does not require much reflection to show that this doctrine is contrary both to justice and to common sense : it was frequently criticized by judges : yet it remained binding on inferior Courts, until in 1887 the Court of Appeal emphatically overruled it in the case of *The Bernina*, the opinion of the Court being summed up in the unequivocal words of Lord Justice Lopes : "The theory . . . is, in my opinion, a fallacy and a fiction, contrary to sound law and contrary to every principle of justice."

Thus former judgments are from time to time overruled by superior and co-ordinate Courts; but this is done with the greatest caution in England, because it is recognized that it is not only important to find the right solutions of legal problems, but also to keep to solutions once obtained in order not to confuse the public and the legal profession. Indeed it has been said with some exaggeration that in law certainty is more important than justice.

It may be added, however, that the doctrine as to the binding force of precedents is not a necessary consequence of the theory of case-law. It does not obtain, *e.g.* in the jurisprudence of the Privy Council in England and of the Supreme Court in the United States. As we have already seen (p. 143) the first decision as to the Legal Tender Act was reversed later on. Besides, even in English common law the systematic use of precedents is a comparatively late development, and as late as the nineteenth century, the keystone of the whole structure—the uniformity of practice in the House of Lords—was not yet established. About 1850 such legal authorities as Lord St. Leonards and Lord Campbell held opposite views on the matter.[1] The first said, in *Bright* v. *Hutton* (1852):

"Although you are bound by your own decisions as much as any Court would be bound, so that you could not reverse your decision in a particular case, yet you are

[1] See Pollock, *First Book of Jurisprudence.*

M

not bound by any rule of law you may lay down, if upon subsequent occasion you find reason to differ from that rule; that is, that this court, like every court of justice, possesses an inherent power to correct an error into which it may have fallen."

This was contested by Lord Campbell, who often had occasion to assert what became the received view on the subject.

Still, it is only under this system of binding precedents that the necessary continuity and certainty inherent in the conception of law can be achieved on the basis of judicial decisions.

2. Cases are seldom exactly similar. Certain differences in the circumstances may make it a matter of difficulty to apply precisely an existing standard. When a Court refers to precedent, it generally has to use reasoning in order to show that in spite of minor differences a principle stated in a former case can be applied to a later one; and sometimes this can only be done by means of rather complicated argument. Such instances bring into strong relief the fact that what is important in the precedent is not the actual decision, but the principle on which it is grounded, or,

as it is technically called, the *ratio decidendi*. This may either be explicitly stated by the Court in deciding the case, or may have to be discovered by close examination of the judgment. In either case, it will be regarded as authoritative in subsequent cases. It may be said, therefore, that a judge who formulates a principle of decision in a dispute, if he does not simply repeat what has been established by a predecessor on a similar occasion, formulates a rule of law.

A peculiar difficulty in English and American cases arises from the fact that the decision is formulated by each member of the Court separately, and not by the Court as a whole. Therefore, although the concrete question at issue is always definitely decided, the principle of the decision may be differently expressed, and even differently conceived, by the various members of the Court. Let us take an example from a recent and a famous case.[1] It is well known that Osborne, a member of the Amalgamated Society of Railway Servants, refused to contribute to the political funds collected by this trade union, as well as by others, for the maintainance of the Labour

[1] *Osborne* v. *Amalgamated Society of Railway Servants* (1910).

Party in Parliament. When the case came up in due course before the House of Lords, such levies for political purposes by trade unions were declared illegal : but the reason for this declaration was not formulated definitely by the Court, and as a matter of fact, the five lords who sat in this case came to the ultimate conclusion on different grounds. Two, Lord Halsbury and Lord Macnaghten, clearly based their decision on the view that the objects of a trade union are restricted to the three mentioned in clause 16 of the Trade Unions Act of 1876 : that the political pressure exerted by a trade union on members of Parliament was not among them, and could not be treated as an incidental and subordinate aim. On the other hand, Lord Shaw and Lord James of Hereford expressed the opinion that the above-mentioned clause could not be treated as an exhaustive enumeration of the objects of a trade union. In their view, the illegality consisted in the pledge imposed on members of Parliament to follow a certain line prescribed by the Labour Party. Lord Atkinson agreed in substance with Lord Halsbury and Lord Macnaghten : and if it had been necessary to summarize the considerations of the judges in a single decision,

there would have been a majority of three
against two in regard to the principle that the
action described was beyond the powers of
the union as formulated in the Act of 1876.
As a matter of fact, the decision of the Court
was not reduced to such a unity of principle,
and the different members were left, in this
case as in so many others, to give a varying
colour to their common decision. This peculiarity of English law makes it somewhat difficult
to evolve the principles of decision in many
cases; but of course it does not fundamen-
tally alter the process by which such decisions
are arrived at. Sometimes, however, hardship is inflicted on litigants, and an unsatisfactory and contradictory state of the law
produced, by a division of judicial opinion.
For instance, in the case of *Jolly* v. *Kine*
(1907), an important point arose in connection
with certain ancient lights : in the Court of
Appeal, judgment went against the appellant,
but only by majority, Lord Justice Romer
dissenting; in the House of Lords, the Court
consisted of four Lords only : the Lord Chancellor (Lord Loreburn) and Lord James of
Hereford were in favour of dismissing the
appeal, while Lord Robertson and Lord Atkinson were for allowing it. In such cases of

equal division, the practice of the Court is to
dismiss the appeal (though without costs):
and thus the appellant might not unreason-
ably have said that he had probably lost his
case for no other reason than that the Court
in the House of Lords happened to consist of
an even number of members; and not only
this, but a decision was established under
these unsatisfactory circumstances which, if
the point arises again, may be hard to recon-
cile with a very important authority [*Colls* v.
Home and Colonial Stores (1904)].

3. The principles formulated in precedents
correspond in a system of case-law to the
clauses of a statute in enacted law. In both
cases the problem for the judges may be
compared to the process of logical deduction
which leads to a so-called syllogism the
process of reasoning which is illustrated by
the well-known example, " All men are
mortal (major premise) : Socrates is a man
(minor premise) : therefore Socrates is mortal
(conclusion)." In enacted law, the major
premise of the syllogism is given in a statutory
clause, and the problem is to formulate the
minor premise from which the conclusion is
to be drawn—that is, to analyze the case in
hand in such a way as to bring it under the

operation of the major premise contained in
the clause. The process of bringing the
minor premise under the major premise—
that is to say, of bringing the particular facts
of a case within a general rule—is technically
called *subsumption.*

The application of the Workmen's Compensation Act by the Courts provides many
illustrations of this process. A major premise
is the rule of the Act that workmen or their
families are to be compensated for accidents
arising out of and in the course of the employment.
It is not always easy to fit the minor to the
major premise in order to reach the conclusion
that the employer is liable to compensate.

Suppose, for example, that a sailor, while
returning to his ship from the shore, falls from
the ladder at the ship's side and is drowned.
Do the facts warrant the subsumption of this
case under the major premise of the above-
mentioned rule? In *Moore* v. *Manchester
Liners* (1910) in the House of Lords, three of
the judges held that they did, because " the
danger of falling from a ladder which gave
the only access to the ship is incidental to the
service of a seaman," and because a sailor
returning from leave does so " in the course
of his employment." Two authoritative

judges, Lord Macnaghten and Lord Mersey, were, however, of a different opinion, because they thought that the course of employment had been interrupted by the man going ashore " on his own business."

To take another example : in the case of *Nisbet* v. *Rayne*, to which we have already referred (p. 122), it was held that the accident arose " out of and in the course of " the deceased man's employment, because a murderous attack was a risk peculiarly incident to the duties of a cashier who was in the habit of carrying large sums of money on his person. A later case provides an interesting contrast. In *Mitchinson* v. *Day* (1913), a carter, seeing a drunken man about to interfere with his horse, warned him that he might be injured by the animal : the drunken man then turned upon his would-be benefactor, assaulted and killed him. The Court held that though the accident arose *in the course of* the deceased's employment, it did not, as in the former case, arise *out of* it, for the danger of assault by an intoxicated ruffian was in no sense incident to the calling of a carter. It is further interesting to note, as an example of the force of judicial interpretation, that the construction placed upon the word " accident " in

Nisbet v *Rayne* was accepted as binding authority in the later case, and it was never doubted that the assault and homicide constituted an " accident " within the meaning of the Act. Thus the case really resolved itself into a question of subsumption.

The above case may serve to show how the Courts bring the minor premise of a particular case under the major premise of a statute. Very often the major premise to which the circumstances of a case are to be applied is a rule, not of legislative enactment, but of common law. For example, it is a rule of common law that there can be no theft of wild animals (including wild birds). Let us take an instance of the application of this rule. In *Regina* v. *Cory* (1864), the prisoner was indicted for stealing eighty tame pheasants, which had been hatched by a common hen, and which, as it appeared in evidence, were intended to be turned loose when they were of an age to leave the hen. Now there was no doubt that pheasants were " wild animals " in law, and in their wild state could not be the subjects of larceny : but the question was whether these particular birds, being kept under the control of the prosecutor, could be considered " tame " in the circumstances of this case. Baron Channell, in directing the jury, said : " As a matter of law, I have no difficulty whatever in telling you that these pheasants, having been hatched by hens, and reared in a coop, were tame pheasants at the time they were taken, whatever might have been their destiny afterwards. Being thus, the prosecutor had such a property in them that they would become the subjects of larceny." Thus the judge brought the case within the major premise of common law : and it is worth noting that this application of the major premise by a single judge in a direction to the jury was adopted by a superior Court (the Court of Crown Cases Reserved) in the later and important case of *Regina* v. *Shickle* (1868).

Thus we see that in the process of case-law judges have often to bring the minor premise of a particular case within a well-defined major premise either of statute or of common law. But sometimes their task is more difficult. They have to discover the major premise itself before they can determine the rule under which the case falls. Suppose I keep on my land a very large accumulation of water which, if it escapes, is practically certain to do damage to others. If it does in fact escape, and an action is brought, the major premise is not, or rather was not, altogether clear. The question is whether I shall be liable only if the water escapes through my negligence : or whether, having taken the responsibility of keeping a particularly dangerous object on my land for my own purposes, I must be held liable whether its escape was due to my negligence or not. This was the problem which faced the Court in the celebrated case of *Rylands* v. *Fletcher* (1868). The facts of the case may be given in the words of Lord Moulton in a recent judgment [1]:

"The defendants . . . had constructed a reservoir on their land to collect and hold water for the purpose of working their mill. Under that land were situated underground workings of an abandoned coal mine, the existence of which was unknown to everybody. After the reservoir had been filled, the water found its way down to those underground workings through some old shafts, and escaping through them flooded the plaintiff's colliery. The defendants had been guilty of no negligence either in the construction or the use of the reservoir, and

[1] *Rickards* v. *Lothian* (1913), A.C. at p. 275.

they contended that in the absence of negligence they were not liable. The plaintiff contended on the other hand that the defendants, having brought and stored the water upon their land for their own purposes, were bound to keep it safely there, and that if it escaped to adjoining lands and did damage the defendants were liable for the breach of this duty whether or not it was due to negligence."

The Court had to discover the major premise under which the case should be brought: it had to reason by analogy from the liability for other kinds of dangerous things, *e.g.* wild animals: and finally it set up the principle (in the words of Mr. Justice Blackburn, subsequently approved by the House of Lords) that "the person who for his own purposes brings on his lands and collects and keeps there anything likely to do mischief if it escapes, must keep it in at his peril, and if he does not do so, is *prima facie* answerable for all the damage which is the natural consequence of its escape." In other words, the Court set up the major premise of what is generally, though not universally, recognized as the "doctrine of absolute liability."

4. When a new principle has been formulated by the judges, their decision on the case assumes authority, and if this authority is followed on subsequent occasions the case is called a leading case. I will borrow an example from a recent writer on Jurisprudence [1] :

" In the year 1620, the Court of King's Bench decided the famous case of *Pells* v. *Brown*. It was this : Land was devised to Thomas Brown and his heirs, but if he died without issue in the lifetime of his brother William, the land was to go to William and his heirs; that is, Thomas took an estate in fee simple, with an executory devise, as it is called, over to William, in case Thomas should die in the lifetime of William without issue. Thomas parted with the land by a conveyance, . . . and the question was whether Edward Pells, who claimed the land under this conveyance, held it subject to the executory devise to William or free from it, or, in other words, whether an executory devise after a fee simple is destructible by the holder of the fee.

" The Court, by three judges to one, decided that the executory devise continued, that Pells took the land subject to it, that Thomas

[1] J. C. Gray.

could not destroy it; and so the law has been held ever since. Therefore, in England and America future contingent interests can be validly created by will. This is by no means a necessary state of things. In Germany, in France, in Louisiana, and generally, I believe, where the Civil Law prevails, future contingent interests are allowed, if at all, only to a very limited extent."

5. In a series of cases connected with some particular legal principle, it often happens that the original authority is gradually modified by practice : it is expanded or contracted according to the coming in of new circumstances, and also by the influence of new considerations arising out of the progress of opinion both among the public at large and among the professional class of lawyers. All these features are of such importance both practically and theoretically that I should like to call attention to one or two characteristic instances.

Lawyers are exceedingly averse from treating original principles as entirely new or invented rules. It is only in the sphere of the equity jurisdiction of Chancery, which for historical reasons has been less trammelled by precedents than that of the common law

Courts, that the process of invention has been distinctly avowed. But it is evident that the same process has really been operating in the history of common law as in equity : for how could the huge body of common law doctrines have been evolved if the judges had not had power to formulate legal rules when the statutory law of the country did not provide express legislation? The study of the actual practical course of English legal development leads to the same conclusion.

Not long ago the following case was tried at the Manchester Assizes.[1] The action was brought by an infant of the age of four years, suing by his father as his next friend, to recover damages for personal injuries alleged to have been caused by the negligence of a servant of the defendant corporation. An automatic gas-meter in the house of the plaintiff's father having got out of order in consequence of a coin being jammed in it, a postcard was sent to the town hall complaining of the defect and asking that some one might be sent to put it right. By some mistake this complaint was not attended to, but the plaintiff's nurse seeing in the street a man named Ford, who was an inspector of gas=

[1] *Forsyth* v. *Manchester Corporation* (1912).

fittings in the employment of the defendant corporation, and was wearing the uniform of the gas department, asked him to come and look at the meter. Ford accordingly went in and attempted to remedy the defect by the use of his pocket-knife. Failing in this, he went out to get some proper tools, and left the knife open somewhere in the room which contained the meter. While he was absent the plaintiff played with the knife and ran it into his eye, which ultimately had to be removed.

The plaintiff's case was that in leaving the knife where the child had access to it Ford had been guilty of negligence, and that, the negligence having been committed in the course of his employment, the corporation was liable in damages. The defendants alleged that Ford in doing what he did was not acting within the scope of his authority, he being an inspector of gas-fittings and not a repairer of meters. The jury found Ford guilty of negligence while acting in the course of his employment, and awarded £125 damages. The judge, however, ordered judgment to be entered for the defendants, being of opinion that there was no evidence to support the finding that Ford was acting in the course of his employment. The plaintiff naturally

appealed, but the Court of Appeal upheld
the decision of the Court below.   Lord Justice
Vaughan Williams said, among other things,
that in his judgment it was quite plain that the
duty of this inspector was merely to inspect
and report, and there was no evidence whatever that in attempting to remove with his
knife the coin which was jammed in the meter
he was acting within the scope of his authority.
It seemed to him that this attempt was
nothing more than a piece of volunteer
kindness.

This case may be taken as characteristic
of the present state of the doctrine of the
responsibility of masters for the acts of their
employees. Now, this doctrine must be
traced historically through a series of stages
from a time when the common law of the
kingdom considered the question from a
point of view opposite to that which is accepted now. All through the mediæval period,
as reflected in the Year Books, the view prevailed that a master is responsible for *any*
wrongs committed by his servant in the
course of his employment. In the sixteenth
century the Courts began to recognize that it
was unfair to put such a wide construction on
the liability of the master, and the doctrine
N

of *general employment* was modified by the requirements of *particular authority* on the part of the master. This means that " the master in order to be liable must have commanded the very act in which the wrong consisted." Towards the end of the seventeenth century a reaction set in. " The nation was reaping in commercial fields the harvest of prosperity sown in the Elizabethan age and destined to show fullest fruition in the age of Anne. The conditions of industry and commerce were growing so complicated, and the original undertaker and employer might now be so far separated from the immediate doer, that the decision of questions of masters' liability must radically affect the conduct of business affairs in a way now for the first time particularly appreciated " (J. H. Wigmore).

It came to be assumed that masters and employers were responsible for the acts of their servants and employees in so far as the latter could be held to have acted by their express or *implied command*. This is the view followed by the Courts under the influence of judgments of Lord Holt and Lord Hardwicke in the eighteenth century. In order to meet the complicated requirements of growing industry and commerce, the chief stress was laid on determining how far an agent was acting for his master's business or benefit; this became the test of an *implied command,* and the master's responsibility for torts committed by the agent was co-extensive with the authority which he was deemed to have given. Lastly, about 1800 the doctrine assumed its modern shape, chiefly through the action of Lord Kenyon as Chief Justice of the King's Bench. The test of responsibility came to be expressed in the words " within the scope of the employment," the very words which were used in the recent judgment at Manchester. Thus we see that the law as to the responsibility of masters and employers has passed through four stages of development, and that it was elaborated by means of decisions of the Courts under the influence of changing conditions and opinions.[1]

Altogether, the gradual modification of rules once accepted as conclusive authority affords an interesting insight into the cross-currents of public opinion and legal doctrine. The class of lawyers, and especially the judges who assume the direct responsibility for the

---

[1] On the whole subject see J. H. Wigmore : *Responsibility for Tortious Acts*, in *Anglo-American Essays in the History of English Law*, pp. 520 ff.

settlement of disputes involving immense prac‑
tical interests, cannot afford to disregard the
change of views taking place in the ranks of
society at large in regard to fundamental
problems of law. Such questions, for instance, as the extent of criminal responsibility,
the modes and degrees of punishment, the
civil rights of married and unmarried women,
the position of children under the disciplinary
power of parents, are sure to excite a great
deal of feeling among the public, and the
results of conflicting views are bound to vary
a great deal from age to age. The movement
of judicial case-law is bound to follow to some
extent these currents of opinion, although
they will in some degree be moderated by the
conservative traditions of tribunals : as it
has been wittily put by Professor Dicey, the
views of judges are apt to correspond to the
opinions of the day before yesterday.

6. The conservative and traditional leanings
of the lawyer's mind are expressed, even in
such cases, by the fact that the Courts lean
in the absence of direct precedent on statements of doctrine in books,[1] and on maxims,

[1] For example : In Mr. Justice Walton's judgment in
Prested Miners' Gas Indicating Electric Lamp Company v.
Gardner (1910), the view that s. 4 of Statute of Frauds

that is, on general propositions of law derived from treatises, lectures, pronouncements of foreign jurists, etc. It is to a great extent in this indirect way that Roman Law has come to exercise a strong influence on the development of English Law. Counsel did not quote the Corpus Juris, and Courts never grounded their decision on clauses from the Digest or the Codex; but general propositions evolved from the study of Roman Law were constantly circulated in the course of trials, and sometimes endorsed and construed by the judges. It was, for example, a maxim of Roman Law that no action will lie on any agreement entered into for immoral purposes (*ex injusta causa non oritur actio*),[1] and we see this principle reproduced in English Law. In *Scott* v. *Brown* (1892) an action was brought by the plaintiff against the defendants, who were stockbrokers, for the rescission of a contract to purchase shares in a certain company which, at the time of the making of the contract, had not been brought out, and to

may apply to the sale of goods was set up largely on the strength of opinions expressed in Smith's *Leading Cases* and in Leake's *Contracts*.

[1] Dig. II, 14, 2 : *Pacta quae turpem causam continent non sunt observanda.*

recover money paid to the defendants for the said shares, on the ground that the defendants while acting as the plaintiff's brokers had delivered their own shares to him instead of purchasing them on the Stock Exchange at a premium in accordance with the agreement; the object of this transaction being to induce the public to believe that there were buyers of such shares at a premium on the Stock Exchange, when in fact there were none but the plaintiff.   In the Court of Appeal, Lord Justice Lindley said that the maxim *ex turpi causa non oritur actio* (an action cannot arise from an immoral consideration)

" expresses a clear and good legal principle which is not confined to indictable offences. No Court ought to enforce an illegal contract or allow itself to be made a means of enforcing such obligations alleged to arise out of a contract or transaction which is illegal, if the illegality is duly brought to the notice of the Court, and if the person invoking the aid of the Court is himself implicated in the illegality."   [The plaintiff shows that he wished to deceive the public.   His purchase was an actual purchase.]   " Under these circumstances the plaintiff must look else-

where than in a court of justice for such
assistance as he may require if the claim
to such assistance is based on his illegal
contract."

Eventually a body of conveniently stated
rules arose which could not always be traced
directly either to Roman Law or to precedent, but which served as a guide for parties
and judges in litigation. Of course their
legal authority has to be distinguished carefully from their doctrinal or literary history :
legal authority could be imparted to them
only by their recognition in the courts for
the purpose of formulating the principle of
the decision (*ratio decidendi*) in given cases.

7. The literary treatment of legal topics by
writers who desire either to state and explain
existing rules, or to systematize them, or to
offer criticisms and suggest alterations or to
discuss particular problems and cases, cannot
in itself constitute a source of law. Its aim
is the expression of ideas entertained by one
or the other jurist, but not the promulgation
of rules obligatory for any one else. But there
may be and there have actually been cases
when the opinions of experts who were neither
legislators nor judges was appealed to, and

obtained authoritative force. The most conspicuous instance of this is afforded by the
consultations of authorities in the jurisprudence (*responsa prudentium*) of Roman
Law. In difficult cases Roman magistrates
of the early period consulted the pontifices as
to legal rules, and later on asked famous
lawyers for their advice. Parties to a suit
also obtained private consultations, which
were sometimes accepted as authoritative by
a tribunal. From the time of Augustus the
right to give such consultations (*jus respon-
dendi*) began to be conferred officially by the
Emperor on certain leading jurists. In course
of time not only direct *responsa* in a given
case, but *responsa* obtained in former cases
and passages from the writings of famous
jurisconsults began to be quoted as authorities. It is not quite clear, however, in what
way conflicts of opinion were solved in the
earlier empire. Valentinian III tried to
settle difficulties arbitrarily by selecting
five especially authoritative jurists whose
writings and opinions were to prevail, and by
allowing a kind of casting vote to Papinian
among these five. But obviously such an
expedient was insufficient to get rid of all
difficulties. Papinian might be silent on the

very question in dispute, and opinions of deceased writers could not always be mechanically arrayed against each other. It is clear that the judgment and discretion of the judges before whom the actual case was tried must have played a considerable part in the selection of suitable authorities. Justinian tried to find a way out of confusion by reducing the opinions of legal writers to a compendium in his digest. It cannot be said that this enterprise was altogether a success, for all sorts of obscurities and contradictions were still left to be cleared up. But the Digest in any case marks the close of a period when writers on jurisprudence were referred to as authorities for the formulation of legal rules and the collection of fragments from their books took the shape of clauses in a code. It is the preceding period that is chiefly of interest for our purpose. The peculiarity of the method lies in the fact that the judges, instead of formulating legal rules by the help of their own minds, as in judge-made law, turn to the assistance of writers or consulting jurists. The latter perform the same kind of mental operations as a Court would have to perform when settling case-law; but there is a division between jurisprudential and judicial authority, though the boundary between the two is not clearly traced, at least as regards the decision of the concrete case. And the doctrinal analysis assumes the character of a legal source not by its own weight, but because it is adopted in one way or another by the Emperor or by the magistrate. It must therefore be regarded as preparing either of case-law or of legislation, according to its contents and the circumstances in which it was given.

The use of the gloss to the Corpus Juris during the later Middle Ages as well as during the sixteenth and seventeenth centuries is another instance of the direct authority of jurisprudential doctrine. The proverb " *Che non ha Azzo non vade al palazzo*," [1] may be taken as a practical hint as to the best manual of positive law; but there is also the doctrine " What is not received in the commentary of the glossators is not received by the tribunal " (" *quod non agnoscit glossa non agnoscit forum* "), which shows that the ordinary commentary to the Corpus, the glossa of Accursius, which was a kind of compendium of the writings of glossators, was used as a

---

[1] " He who has not a copy of Azzo's books need not go to the Courts of Justice."

means to limit to some extent the body of rules which could be pleaded in the Courts of Italy and Germany, where references to Civil Law were admitted. In a sense the Corpus Juris itself, as the basis of the so-called common law received in Germany before the introduction of the new Civil Code of that country, was a law of the learned : and this explains the curious practice, much followed by Courts, of sending up the documents of a case to the Law Faculty of a University of some standing—Halle, Greifswald, Jena—in order to obtain a consultation as to the proper decision. This appeal to private authority is in a great measure akin to the submission of parties to private arbitration. It testifies to a rather helpless state of the Courts themselves, and must be considered exceptional.

8. Case-law cannot be brought under the operation of a famous doctrine proclaimed for enacted law, namely, that it ought not to have retroactive application. This principle has been emphatically asserted in the Constitution of the United States, and has given rise to decisions of the Supreme Court which invalidate laws passed by single States and even by Congress. Conspicuous instances of this kind occur in connection with the Civil War in the

'sixties. In *Cummings* v. *Missouri*, the State of Missouri had passed a clause in its Constitution in 1865 requiring from all who held or took certain specified offices and honours an oath to the effect that the taker of it had never been hostile, or supported those hostile, to the United States or to the Government. Cummings, a Roman Catholic priest, was indicted under this law for teaching and preaching without having taken the necessary oath. He was fined and committed to jail until the fine was paid. In due course his case came up before the Supreme Court of the United States, which decided by majority that the law was invalid as inflicting penalties for acts which at the time they were committed were not illegal : in other words, it was in effect an " *ex post facto* " law prohibited by the federal constitution.

In a similar way in *Ex parte Garland* (1866), the Supreme Court invalidated a law of Congress in consequence of which an advocate was prevented from pleading before the Supreme Court because he had taken part in the rebellion.

It is impossible to apply this doctrine to judge-made law without resorting to a fiction, for if a case is material for an enunciation of law, the application of this very law to this very case is necessarily retroactive. The parties could not know what the law was before the decision was given, and it is the exact knowledge which makes all the difference in a dispute : no one would willingly expose himself to defeat and heavy costs if he knew for certain that the law was against him. The most bitter criticism of the uncertainty of the methods of English common law has been offered by Bentham :

" On the question what the law is, so long as the rule of action is kept in the state of common, alias unwritten, alias imaginary law, authority is everything. The question is what on a given occasion A (the judge) is likely to think : wait till your fortune has been spent in the inquiry, and you will know; but forasmuch as it is naturally a man's wish to be able to give a guess on what the result will eventually be, before he has spent his fortune . . . he applies, through the medium of B (an attorney) for an opinion to C (a counsel), who, considering what D (a former judge) has said or been supposed to say, deduces therefrom his guess as to what, when the time comes, judge A, he thinks, will say " (VIII, 397).

Without putting the case in this caustic way, we have to recognize that sometimes on very important points of law the highest authorities will take opposite views.

Sometimes the uncertainty as to the state of the common law may be so great that some of the judges may dissent from the decision of their colleagues, and a Court below may pronounce its judgment in one sense while a Court above may come to exactly the opposite conclusion. Thus in the Taff Vale case already mentioned (p. 81), Mr. Justice Farwell held the trade union to be liable for torts committed by its agents : the Court of Appeal held the opposite opinion; but ultimately the House of Lords laid down that the trade union should be put on the footing of a corporation and should therefore be liable.

This is an unavoidable consequence of the case-law system, but it has a deeper meaning than may appear at first sight. It is a result of the fact that in the process of the making of law by judges, the law appears not as the formulation of a command followed by execution, but as a declaration of existing right obtained through the wisdom and learning of the judges. The material rather than the formal side of legal rules comes to the fore.

It is not absolutely necessary for the settlement of disputes that prospective commands should have been given, but it is absolutely necessary that there should be means of ascertaining what is, in the opinion of persons provided with judicial authority, the way to settle the difficulty in a manner most consonant with right and justice.   In other words, the decision, before it can become an authority, must be a definite *declaration of right.* This by itself should be sufficient to show the defective character of the current Austinian definition, and it is surprising that this truth has not been realized more fully by English jurists; for the common law, with which they have principally to deal, stands or falls with the admission of legal principles obtained not by command, but by retrospective estimates of right and justice.

CHAPTER VIII

1. WE have discovered by this time how large a part in the formulation of law is played by judicial declarations of right in the process of interpretation of statutes as well as in the formation of custom and of case-law. But there is a fourth legal source in which the creative power of Courts is even more conspicuous, because it has to be exercised to a great extent in opposition to recognized legal rules. This is *Equity*, or fairness. The equity I am speaking of now is not the modern equity jurisdiction of English tribunals, which has been combined with common law by the Judicature Acts of 1873–5, and which even for some hundred and fifty years before that event, since the times of Lords Chancellors Nottingham, Hardwicke and Eldon, had assumed the character of a legal system as technical as common law itself, although sometimes conflicting with the common law in a curious way

Modern English equity is interesting for our purpose only in so far as its peculiar course has been shaped historically by the operation of principles distinct from ordinary legal rules. But it is in the earlier history of this branch of English law, in the period ranging roughly from the fourteenth to the eighteenth centuries, that we get the best material for a study of equity as a distinct principle. Roman history and the observation of the legal institutions of the Greeks, the Germans, and other nations also give excellent illustrations of the process under discussion.

One important point was noticed and explained by Aristotle: he calls attention to the fact that legal rules are necessarily general, while the circumstances of every case are particular, and that it is beyond the power of human insight and science to lay down in advance rules which will fit all future variations and complications of practice. Therefore law must be supplemented by equity (*epieikeia*); there must be a power of adaptation and flexible treatment, sometimes suggesting decisions which will be at variance with formally recognized law, and yet will turn out to be intrinsically just.

o

The same principle has been put forward in very distinct terms in the Introduction to the French Code of 1804.

In the practice of Roman law during the last centuries of the Republic and the early period of the empire, we often hear of an opposition between the spirit and the letter of the law. Cicero's speeches furnish us with an excellent example of a struggle between equitable and formalistic interpretation in the process between Caecina and Aebutius. There was a dispute between two Romans of high rank, A. Caecina and L. Aebutius, about a certain estate. As a step in the legal procedure appropriate to the case, it was necessary for Caecina to make a formal entry upon the land; this he attempted to do, but was prevented by Aebutius, who opposed him with a force of armed men. Without trying conclusions by force, Caecina brought an action against Aebutius in the form of a so-called interdict (*unde vi armata*) This interdict applied to the violent dispossession of a landowner, and was framed as follows : " In the place whence thou or thy slaves or agent hast this year violently ousted him or his slaves or agent from possession in that place do thou reinstate him in possession." When the case came up for trial, the defendant objected, among other things, that as a matter of fact there had been no ejectment and no violence. Cicero, as counsel for the plaintiff, retorted by ridiculing the view that the law did not apply except in cases of actual ejectment and violence in the literal sense of the words. " It is as if the defendant said," he urged, " ' Yes, I have done these things, and you have no means of proceeding against me by civil action before the Praetor.' When our ancestors were men of such diligence and prudence as to establish every requisite law not only for such important cases as this, but for even the most trivial matters, will you hold that they overlooked this class of cases, the most important of all, so that, if people had compelled me to depart from my home by force of arms, I should have had a right of action, but as they only prevented me from entering my home, I have none? Shall that man gain his cause before your tribunal, who defends himself by this argument, ' I drove you *away* with armed men, but I did not drive you *out* ' ? "

Turning to the question of actual violence, Cicero continues : " Aebutius is not touched by this interdict, because violence was not offered to Caecina. Can you then, Aebutius, say that it was not violence which hindered him, when by reason of an armed force he was unable to come to a place, when he wished to come there and had gone out with that intention? What then shall we say? If he had been there, and if under the influence of fear he had fled from that place when he saw the armed men, would you then say that he had been driven away? I think so. Will you judges, then, who decide disputes with such care and such subtlety, by expressions and not by equity, you who interpret laws . . . by their letter, will you be able to say that a man has been driven away, who has never been touched? What! Will you say that he has been thrust out from his place? For that was the word that the Praetors formerly used in their interdicts. Can any one be thrust out who is not touched? Must we not if we abide by the strict letter, understand that that man only is thrust out on whom hands are laid? What law, what resolution of the Senate, what treaty cannot be invalidated and torn to pieces if we choose to bend facts to words and leave out of the question the intention and design and authority of those who wrote them ? "

Again, the requirements of the ever growing Imperial jurisdiction of Rome led to the development of a special system of law for the relations of subjects who were not Roman citizens. The foreign praetor (*praetor peregrinus*) and the proconsuls had to elaborate and to apply legal principles different from those which were current between citizens, and thus the *jus gentium* arose by the side of the national *jus civile* as a body of general rules of law suggested by fairness, common sense, knowledge of the world and some acquaintance with foreign law. The magistrates who were entrusted with jurisdiction in these cases based their decisions and the prospective rules of their edicts on general considerations of equity and utility (*ex bono et aequo*).

The recognition of the value of these principles in regard to foreigners reacted powerfully on the situation of the citizens themselves. It was not to be expected that Romans would continue to submit to narrow and rigid forms when a wider and wiser treatment of legal problems had been evolved for their subjects. And as a matter of fact the jurisdiction of the city praetor was soon modified in the same direction as that of the *praetor peregrinus* and of the provincial governors.

One of the fundamental principles which governed the rules of succession in the strict law of Rome was *agnation*, that is, relationship based either on kinship through the male stock, or on artificial adoption into the family according to prescribed legal forms. The usual successor to an estate came from the class of so-called " own heirs," or members of the family under the immediate " power " of the father. In a case of intestacy, these " own heirs " were first entitled to the inheritance; after them came the nearest agnatic relative of the deceased. The rigid application of these rules imposed material hardships on persons who came to be considered as having a natural right to share in the property of the deceased; and the praetor therefore mitigated the severity of their operation by applying the principles of the law of nations. This he effected by developing the doctrine of " possession of the estate " (*bonorum possessio*). He did not override or abrogate the rules of the strict law, nor did he destroy the legal title of the heir; but by the employment of fictions and summary remedies he placed " *in the position* of heir " a person whom he considered to have a natural claim. In cases of intestacy he supplemented the principle of agnation by the wider principle of *cognation,* or blood kinship in the modern sense, including, of course, relationship on the female side. Preference was given firstly to legitimate children of the deceased; secondly, to those entitled by the strict legal rules of succession; thirdly, to nearest kindred in blood; and fourthly, to the widow or widower of the deceased.

2. An analogous process took place in English law when the writ procedure and substantive common law had attained to their full development in the course of the thirteenth century and early half of the fourteenth. The beneficial effects of a technically developed law had been inestimable for England, securing for her a considerable superiority in civil order over Germany and even France. But, towards the middle of the fourteenth century, the common law was in danger of becoming entangled in professional technicalities and losing touch with the social requirements of the nation. The free handling of legal institutions, the

creative power of leading judges in framing
and developing rules of law, began to de-
generate; the rigid framing of the writs and
the sophistic methods of pleading hampered
the great progressive movement which had
given birth to the remarkable jurisprudence
of the Courts of Henry III and of Edward I.
The " actions on the case " inaugurated by
the Statute Westminster II had not quite
borne the fruits which might have been
expected from this form of procedure. It
was at this critical period that the Court of
Chancery came forward with fresh impulses,
under the influence of the foreign learning
of Canon and of Roman law, and supported
by the recognition of conscience as one of
the sources of legal action. I need not go
into details of the interesting history of
Chancery jurisdiction. It played a decisive
part, in modifying the status of servile
peasantry and of the villeins, in creating
trusts and in protecting informal agreements.

It is sufficient for my present purpose to
call attention to the first of these points.
Mediæval peasants, the so-called villeins, had
been deprived of protection by the State
in their dealings with their lords. If any
of them complained of being ejected from

his tenure, or of being oppressed by arbitrary exactions on the part of the lord, he was met by the answer that the King's Courts did not interfere in matters concerning the relations between lords and villeins. Now this state of affairs was altered in consequence of a change of views in the Courts. Some time during the fifteenth century, royal judges began to entertain suits brought by peasants against their lords. The problem is when and how this change was brought about. We know now that it was initiated by the exercise of equity in the Court of Chancery. In the fifteenth century a considerable number of cases came before the Court of Chancery. In the sixteenth century the same business, which in view of the number of copyholders must have been a lucrative one, came before the common law Courts.[1]

From 1439 onwards a stream of equitable jurisdiction flows out from the Chancery to secure the title of the very class which has hitherto had no legal title at all. Tenure in villeinage becomes copyhold.

3. It is unnecessary in a sketch of general

[1] See Tawney, *Agrarian Problem in the Sixteenth Century.* pp. 310, etc.

jurisprudence to trace the stages of the momentous conflict between the Courts of common law and the Courts of Equity. This subject belongs properly to the history of English law. But what I should like to point out in this connection is the fact that in spite of modern attempts to harmonize equitable and legal jurisdiction, and in spite of the compromise effected after centuries of rivalry, it has not always been easy to co-ordinate the action of both principles. In a general way it was assumed that " equity follows the law," and that the novelties which it admits are derived from the fact that it provides remedies in cases where the common law does not grant them. This view was, for instance, fully explained by Lord Hardwicke in *Garth* v. *Cotton* (1753). Sometimes, however, an antagonism between the Courts actually found expression in pronouncements of judges. In *Dixon* v. *Gayfere* (1853) the Court of Chancery took a line in regard to the legal effects of possession which was avowedly opposed to a doctrine admitted in common law Courts. The King's Bench retorted in *Asher* v. *Whitlock* (1865) with a declaration of Chief Justice Cockburn that the decision of the Master of the Rolls in *Dixon* v.

Gayfere, however right in equity, was not right in law. The Judicature Acts (1873–5) have put an end to this antagonism, but the difference in the methods of juridical reasoning are still existent and represent, as it were, the opposite poles of practical jurisprudence.

The antagonism we have noticed is to be attributed not merely to a difference of personal opinions, or to a rivalry of institutions, but rather to a fundamental difference of methods. In one system the centre of gravity lies in the formulated rule, and therefore there is a strong tendency to sacrifice the particular to the general, justice to certainty : while in the other there is a more direct quest after right and a wide discretionary power on the part of the judge to draw on his own notions of what is fair and just.

Sir G. Jessel, Master of the Rolls, has said [*Re Hallet's Estate* (1880)] :

" The rules of Equity are not, like the rules of the common law, supposed to be established from time immemorial. It is perfectly well known that they have been established from time to time — altered, improved and refined from time to time. In many cases we know the names of the Chancellors who invented them. No doubt they were invented for the purpose of securing the better administration of justice, but still, they were invented. Take such things as these—the separate use of a married woman, the restraint on alienation, the modern rule against perpetuities, and the rules of equitable waste. We can name the Chancellor who first invented them, and state the date when they were first introduced into equity jurisprudence; and therefore in cases of this kind the older precedents have very little value. The doctrines are progressive, refined and improved, and if we want to know what the rules of Equity are, we must look, of course, rather to the more modern than the more ancient cases."

As there are few enacted laws in primitive societies, and the binding tradition of case-law is not much developed on account of the difficulty of recording precedents and the lack of professional training of the lawyers, the province of discretionary justice is naturally very extensive, and legal progress consists

in a great measure in the substitution of
fixed rules, either legislative or judge-made,
for his fluctuating state of the law. But
it would be wrong to conclude from this
process that the sphere of legal rules is constantly growing at the expense of the sphere
of discretionary justice. A movement in the
opposite direction is also noticeable in all
healthy communities possessed of a strong
feeling for living law. Strict legal rules are
supplemented by allowing a wide margin of
discretion to the judges for their construction,
development, adaptation to circumstances,
and even for their gradual organic modification. Thus equity appears not only as the
most ancient but also as the most modern
form of legal action. The German Civil Code
of 1900 very often employs general statements of various legal principles, with a view
to their differentiation by practice. It commonly refers, for instance, to good faith
(*Treu und Glauben*), business practice, etc.
Any attempt to get rid of this contradictory
tendency in the evolution of law would
speedily reduce legal systems to hopeless
formalism and intolerable pedantry. The
great problem consists in keeping the function of this important element of flexible

equity proportionate to the elements of certainty and stable tradition which are characteristic of the purely legal side of the evolution. A capricious treatment of statutes and leading precedents by the Courts would prove quite as destructive of justice as a rigid application of obsolete rules. The sense of caution in this respect is sometimes strongly expressed by jurists. Application of law in this as in so many other cases is a matter not only of exact knowledge, but of art : all depends on the sense of due proportion in a wise combination of two distinct tendencies.

4. I should like in conclusion to illustrate my view by examples borrowed from Roman and modern English law regarding the three principal functions of equity—the help afforded by the powers of individualization, the supplementing of gaps in law and the correction of harsh consequences of legal rules.[1] The most remarkable instances of equitable individualization—that is, the adaptation of a general rule to particular circumstances—are given by the *responsa* of the great Roman jurists of the second century B.C.   To what far-reaching consequences this power of adaptation

---

[1] *Jus adjuvandi, jus supplendi, jus corrigendi.*

may lead can be seen from the interpretation of testaments and contracts. Roman Law had by the end of the Republic reached the stage when the intention of the testator and of the contracting party is assumed to be the principal factor in the constitution of the testament and of the contract. But in connection with this principle peculiar difficulties arise as regards the right interpretation of such intentions. The ancient formal rule was that the testator's or contracting party's actual words formed the basis of the law in the particular case.[1] But this rule, convenient and simple though it appears, could not always be applied. Words might be obscure and ambiguous; the jurists had to look for their sense, and in doing this they had to be guided by two sets of considerations. To begin with, they might try to ascertain by an attentive study of the context and of probable intentions what the testator or contracting party had wanted to say. Or else they might try to discover what in the given circumstance the testator or contracting party might be reasonably supposed to have intended or ordained. Their minds had to work in one of these two directions

[1] *Uti lingua nuncupasset ita ius esto.*

either by reconstructing the intention of the party, or by imputing to him reasonable motives.

An interesting case occurred in Rome about A.D. 150. One Valerius Nepos had made a will in which, according to law, he had instituted a certain person his heir, and added a number of legacies to various friends, as well as a direction that certain slaves should be emancipated. After a time, however, he changed his mind and struck out the name of the heir. At law, this invalidated the whole will, and the property of the deceased was claimed, in the absence of kindred, by the Treasury. The case came up for decision before the tribunal of the Emperor himself, the great Antoninus Pius. At first sight, there seemed to be no reason for resisting the claim of the Treasury : but the various parties interested in the will were represented by advocates, and the following discussion is recorded to us :

" Zeno : ' I beg, Lord Emperor, that you will hear me with patience : what is your decision with regard to the legacies ? ' The Emperor : ' Do you think that if he struck out the names of the heirs he could have desired the will to stand?' Priscianus, counsel for Leo [evidently one of the beneficiaries under the will]: 'It was only the heirs whose names were struck out.' Longinus, counsel for the Treasury: 'No will which does not appoint an heir can be held valid.' Priscianus: 'The testator did actually emancipate some of his slaves and bequeath certain legacies.' The Emperor commanded everybody to leave the room in order that he might consider the question. When the parties were readmitted, he said: 'This seems to be a case for humane interpretation; we hold therefore that Nepos wished to annul only those directions which he actually struck out.'"

It is clear from the narrative that the Emperor was moved to give his decision by two considerations. He thought that it had been the intention of the testator to remove the name of the instituted heir, but to retain the dispositions in respect of legacies and emancipations. But there was another point: the enlightened opinion of the time was "in favour of liberty," and the Emperor was anxious that the freedmen should not be disappointed. Accordingly, after some

P.

hesitation, he resolved to overlook the flaw in the form of the will, and to interpret it in the spirit of a " humane " equity.

In another characteristic set of cases ordinary rules were individualized by Roman lawyers on the principle that in case of too vague an indication by the law, parties were to act in regard to each other as befits " honourable men " (*ut inter bonos viros agi oporteret*).

5. The second case in which judges have to step in and apply considerations of equity and justice arises when there are obvious gaps in the law. Such cases will often occur in any system of law, and we are by no means insured against them by our civilization and the complexity of our legal arrangements, because new and entirely unforeseen circumstances arise every day in connection with the immense advance of technical invention and of social changes. A great deal of statute law has been, of course, enacted after the introduction of modern scientific improvements, but statutes come generally a long while after the track for them has been cleared by business, and collisions of interests which occur before their promulgation have to be decided on the

strength of general considerations. Courts
are naturally inclined, when they meet with
gaps in the law, to fill them up by the help
of a logical extension of existing doctrines;
but this method does not lead far in the
case of entirely new departures, and progress
is often achieved in such circumstances only
after a good deal of groping in the dark. In
the 'nineties, there was an attempt by English
judges to assimilate motors to traction-
engines for the purposes of law : they had
nothing to guide them in the treatment of
cases concerning motors but the rules in
regard to traction-engines, and even after
the Locomotives Act of 1898 motor-car traffic
was subjected to rules as to speed and management which were very ill-suited to it. In this
way, before the passing of the Motor Cars Act,
1903, magistrates were thrown very much on
their discretion in regard to motor-car traffic.

6. Lastly, we have to consider cases when
equity takes up a standpoint which leads
to downright alterations of existing bad law;
that is, when it acts therefore as a factor
of correction. The history of Roman Law
again gives conspicuous instances of the
gradual amelioration of grossly unjust law
by the conscious and consistent interference

of the Courts. Some of the famous fictions which counteracted the application of obsolete rules were produced in this way. In strict law a Roman spinster had, in default of a testamentary guardian, to be under the guardianship of her father or of the nearest agnate, *i. e.* of the nearest male relation in the male line. This meant that in effect she never came of 'age and could not deal with her property as she chose. But in time it was realized by public opinion that such a state of things produced great hardship. The Courts managed to modify the law without formally abrogating the rule. They achieved this result by protecting women who had contracted a fictitious marriage with some old man from any attempt on the part of this fictitious husband to exercise his rights in practice. It came to this, that the woman got rid of the guardianship of agnates by means of the marriage and was not allowed by the Courts to lapse into subjection to the husband. A similar process took place in the history of English law as regards the property of married women. At common law " Marriage was an assignment of a wife's property rights to her husband during the latter's life." Public opinion became alive to the unfairness and harshness of this rule in the eighteenth century. The Court of Chancery used its doctrines of trusts to modify the obnoxious rules and to enable " a married woman to hold property independently of her husband, and to exert over this property the rights which could be exercised by a man or an unmarried woman."

This success was achieved, after the manner of the best judge-made law, by the systematic and ingenious development of one simple principle, namely, that even though a person might not be able to hold property of his own, it might be held for his benefit by a trustee, whose sole duty it was to carry out the terms of the trust. Hence, as regards the property of married women, came the following results, which were attained only by degrees.

Property given to a trustee for the " separate use " of a woman, whether before or after marriage, is her separate property, that is, it is property which does not in any way belong to the husband. At common law, indeed, it is the property of the trustee, but it is property which he is bound in equity to deal with according to the terms of the trust, and therefore in accordance with the wishes or directions of the woman. Here we have constituted the "separate property," or the "separate estate" of a married woman.

If, as might happen, property was given to or settled upon a woman for her separate use, but no trustee were appointed, then the Court of Chancery further established that the husband himself, just because he was at common law the legal owner of the property, must hold it as trustee for his wife. The Court of Chancery having thus created separate property for a married woman, by degrees worked out to its full result the idea that a trustee must deal with the property of a married woman in accordance with her directions. Thus the Court gave her the power to give away or sell her separate property, as also to leave it to whomsoever she wished by will, and further enabled her to charge it with her contracts. But equity lawyers came to perceive, somewhere towards the beginning of the nineteenth century, that though they had achieved all this, they had not given quite sufficient protection to the settled property of a married woman. Her very possession of the power to deal freely

with her separate property might thwart the
object for which that separate property had
been created; for it might enable a husband
to get her property into his hands. Who
could guarantee that Barry Lyndon might not
persuade or compel his wife to make her
separate property chargeable with his debts,
or to sell it and give him the proceeds?
This one weak point in the defences which
equity had thrown up against the attacks
of the enemy was rendered unassailable by
the astuteness, as it is said, of Lord Thurlow.[1]
He invented the provision, introduced constantly since his time into marriage settle-
ments or wills, which is known as the "restraint on anticipation." This clause, if it
forms part of the document settling property
upon a woman *for her separate use*, makes it
impossible for her during marriage either to
alienate the property or to charge it with her
debts. Whilst she is married she cannot,
in short, in any way anticipate her income,
though in every other respect she may deal
with the property as her own.

Eventually in this, as in many other cases,
the working out of equitable remedies prepared the way for definite legislation, which

[1] See Dicey, *Law and Opinion in England*, p. 375 seq.

was effected by the Married Women's Property Acts, 1882 and 1893.

We may sum up by saying that equity as a method of judicial discretion is inseparable from a complex and efficient system of law. It is not necessary that it should be exercised by special courts, and it does not disappear when special tribunals of equity are merged by a comprehensive reform of the Judicature. The method will retain its value and will have to be exercised in order to supplement the rigidity of prospective general rules.

We have now examined each of the four sources of positive law—legislation, custom, judicial precedents and equity. In practice, important questions may arise as to the way in which these different sources have to be co-ordinated. A general direction as to the principles which should govern this process is to be found in the following clause (cl. 1) of the Swiss Civil Code of 1907—in many respects the best of modern codes. " Legal enactments govern all subjects which they concern either in express words or by inter-pretation. When there is no statutory rule applicable to the case, the judge ought to decide according to customary law. In the

absence of a custom bearing on the point he
ought to decide in conformity with a rule
which he would have formulated if he had
been a lawgiver. In doing so he ought to
follow the views established by jurisprudence
and legal precedents."

CHAPTER IX

THE LAW OF NATURE

1. ALL legal rules are supposed to be reasonable and natural; even the worst have probably some considerations of reason to support them, and the more important doctrines of a legal system generally correspond to some deeply-rooted requirements of society. Even slavery was justified by the Greeks on grounds of the natural inferiority of barbarians and of vanquished nations. In this way it may be rightly said that important rules have a twofold justification, as legal commands and as reasonable propositions. But by saying so much we do not mean that there can be a proper system of law constructed on the basis of pure reason or of " human nature," as opposed to law produced by legislation, judicial decisions or custom. Yet this view has been put forward again and again in the course of history, and it has had a great influence in shaping the development of law.

It has been said rather contemptuously that the law of nature is " jurisprudence in the air " : and the definition need not be repudiated by supporters of this kind of law, for after all the air constitutes one of the most important elements of life, both for good and for evil.

The Greeks were struck by the great variety of positive laws, and asked themselves whether justice and right were only casual arrangements changing with circumstances and times, or whether behind this confusing variety there existed perennial notions of right and wrong, justice and injustice. While sophists and sceptics held the first view, idealistic philosophers from the time of Socrates, Plato and Aristotle maintained the second. In contrast with shifting positive rules, they spoke of unwritten law ingrained in the heart of man, of a common law recurring among different tribes, of a law of nature which reasonable creatures were everywhere bound to recognize; and in Xenophon's reminiscences of Socrates we read that the family relations between man and wife, parents and children, were cited as concrete examples of these ever-recurring rules of the law of nature.

These were speculations of philsophers, but

the great practitioners of law in Rome endorsed them with their authority. They had to deal with numberless legal enactments and customs over which their tribunals exercised sovereign authority. It was not a speculative, but an actual problem for their praetors and proconsuls to reduce this heterogeneous mass to unity and reasonable order. In this way the question of the moral background to changing laws arose in full force, and the Romans eagerly took up the threads of Greek doctrine about a law of nature, as the reasonable basis of all particular laws and more especially of the common law of the empire. Ulpian was inclined to widen the boundaries of this law of nature so as to include even animals : perhaps he took his clue in this respect from the teaching of the Pythagoreans, for whom there was no gulf between animals and man.[1] Others contented themselves with building on the foundations of the rational nature of man, and from this point of view treated a number of legal rules as necessary deductions from reason.

The jurist Paul remarks : " As leases are suggested by nature itself and are to be found

[1] A passage in Xenophon's *Reminiscences of Socrates* may have suggested his examples to him.

in the law of all nations, a particular form of words is not necessary for their validity, but only consent. The same holds good in regard to sale." Wardship, again, is characterized by Gaius (*circ.* A.D. 150) as an institution founded on natural reason, while the compilers of the Institutes under Justinian also speak of natural law in this case. (Gaius, I, 189 : *Inst.* I, 20, 6.)

The tendency of the doctrine was, however, not suggested merely by practical considerations : its strongest elements were derived from philosophical ethics. Men like Papinian and Paul, Antoninus Pius, Marcus Aurelius, were under the sway of stoicism : they saw and worshipped the rule of nature in the world at large; little wonder that they were convinced that reason and right were also the voice of nature, the clearest manifestation of divine power in the world.

In another setting, the same idealistic construction is observed in mediæval jurisprudence where it arose under the influence of Christianity and of the Church. Though according to the teaching of St. Augustine, the City of God is in heaven and the city of the world is a creation of robbers, yet the road to the City of God lay through this world, and mankind had to prepare itself for future life by making the best of the time of trial on earth. God has not forsaken mankind in this trial : He has revealed His law to them and implanted it in their hearts as conscience and reason. The Commonwealths of the earth build up laws of their own which partly serve the purpose of the moral education of men and partly reflect the selfish and sinful purposes of rulers, but in case of conflict men ought to conform to the eternal law of nature of which the Church is the principal interpreter.

Again, after the revival of learning and of secular culture, in the sixteenth, seventeenth, and eighteenth centuries, philosophers deduced a theory of law from a few principles of reason, in the same way as they constructed systems of metaphysics and ethics, of politics and of natural philosophy. With Kant the theory of the law of reason reached its highest point.

2. Sometimes attempts have been made to recognize reason as a source of positive law both in ancient and modern times. The Austrian Code (1811), for example, contains the following clause : " When a case cannot be decided in accordance either with the

words or the spirit of a law, the Court shall take into consideration similar cases decided by law, as well as the motives which suggested other laws of the same kind. Should the case still remain doubtful, it shall be decided in accordance with the law of nature, and with due regard to the circumstances of the case diligently collected and thoroughly considered."

Attempts of this kind to give the theory of the law of nature a direct bearing on the practice of Courts have not been successful, while, on the other hand, the indirect influence of such theories in affecting the opinions of judges and legislators has been very great. The mitigation of slavery in the Roman Empire, *e.g.* may be traced to a change of views expressed, among other things, in the proposition that men are free by nature and that slavery was introduced by the *jus gentium*, the *positive* law common to most nations (as distinct from the *jus naturale*, or natural law).

In the same way doctrines based on the law of nature have had a powerful influence on the formation of International Law, on the reforms of public law in a democratic direction effected by means of the notion of contract, and on the radical alteration of the law of status by the doctrine of equality before the law.

There can be no doubt, for instance, that doctrines about the " rights of man," whatever may be thought of their concrete formulation, have exerted a potent influence on contemporary legal conceptions, and have themselves been derived from speculative doctrines of natural jurisprudence.

In English courts, references to the law of nature have never been favourably considered : but the indirect influence of doctrines based on it has been felt.   In the famous case of the negro slave *Somersett*, which was decided in 1771 (shortly before the secession of the colonies), the slave was claimed by his master, a Virginian planter, while in England. Hargrave, counsel for Somersett, directed part of his argument against the assumption that slavery could be justified by the law of nature. He adopted Locke's reasoning that contract could not be the origin of slavery, because a man cannot divest himself of his right to life or to personal freedom. In regard to conquest and punishment as possible origins of slavery, Hargrave maintained that at the utmost they might justify the enslaving of criminals and of vanquished enemies. But on no account were they sufficient to explain slavery inherited by birth. In giving the judgment which debarred the planter from asserting a right of mastery over the slave, Lord Mansfield declared that " slavery . . . is so odious, that nothing can be suffered to support it, but positive law. Whatever inconveniences," he continued, " may follow from the decision, I cannot say this case is allowed or approved by the law of England; and therefore the black must be discharged."

Another case in which the atmosphere of enlightened rationalism characteristic of the eighteenth century is strongly felt is *Omychund v. Barker* (1744), in which Lord Hardwicke laid it down that heathens might take a legally valid oath according to the ceremonies of their religion, because the essence of an oath is the belief in a Supreme Being capable of rewarding and punishing, and not the particular forms prescribed by Christian confessions.

Thus the law of nature or reason has operated as a literary, but not as a direct, source of law. It is a creation of jurisprudence and philosophy. It is no more a

Q

source of law in the technical sense of the term than the teaching of pandectists or of modern exponents of legal rules. The fact that it has been a most powerful ferment in the evolution of legal ideas does not make it a code to the clauses of which judges can turn in the administration of justice.

It cannot be treated as a code for this simple reason, amongst others, that it is not constant. In reviewing the course of its history, we can easily perceive that in all matters bearing on concrete problems of law it is subject to changes quite as important, if not so frequent and casual, as the changes of positive law. Can one speak, for instance, of a family law based on nature or reason? Would it be based on polygamy, or on strict monogamy as in the Canon Law, or on contractual monogamy, as at present, or on free selection of mates, as may conceivably be the case two or three centuries hence, or on eugenic selection by public authority, as some very advanced sociologists are urging? And is the relation between parents and children clearly prescribed by the law of nature? Children have been in charge of their mothers and under the absolute sway of their fathers, and at the educational disposal of the city

state, and in the temporary care of both
parents. Who knows whether the social
element may not again prevail over the private
organization of education ?   Is property likely
to prove an institution of a perennial law of
nature ?   The origins of property have been
communistic; in its further history it has
been treated more and more from the private,
the individualistic point of view; it cannot
be disputed that socialistic ideas are rapidly
gaining ground in regard to it, that organized
society claims a larger and increasing share in
its distribution and use; can it be maintained that, say, the nationalization of the
land or the monopoly of means of production
by the State would be against the law of
nature ?   People may consider such measures
wrong, dangerous or mischievous, but they
cannot be rejected by a simple appeal to
eternal tenets of the law of reason.   Again,
punishment has certainly been regarded as a
natural sequel to crime by all commonwealths,
although most exalted moralists would have
preferred to reserve punishment to God and
to treat crime as a sin.   But even in the
actual practice of the law, are people agreed
about the aim and scope of punishment ?
Is it a means of repression and amputation

(Plato)? Is it a measure of educational discipline (Aristotle)? Is it principally a deterrent (Bentham)? Is it a necessary moral atonement (Kant)? Is it a measure of medical treatment (Lombroso)? In a word, one has not to go far to perceive that the contents of the law of nature are shifting, and that it would be impossible to reduce it to a unified and permanent code.

Does this mean that the law of nature or reason is a fanciful and absurd misconception? I am afraid the absurdity lies in supposing that a doctrine which has played such a part in the history of the world, which has appealed to minds of men of widely contrasting dispositions in entirely different circumstances, does not rest on solid foundations. Nor is it difficult to see what these foundations are. The law of nature is an appeal from Caesar to a better informed Caesar. It is an appeal by society at large, or by the best spirits of a given society, not against single decisions or rules, but against entire systems of positive law. Legislators are called in to amend law by separate statutes; judges may do a great deal in amending the law by decisions in individual cases, but the wisdom of legislators and the epuity of judges are by themselves powerless against systems, because they start from a recognition of the authority of positive law in general. And yet law, being a human institution, ages not only in its single rules and doctrines, but in its national and historical setting, and the call for purification and reform may become more and more pressing with every generation. Public opinion, then, turns from reality to ideals. Speculation arises as to the essentials of law as conceived in the light of justice. Of course these conceptions of justice are themselves historical, but they are drawn not from the complicated compromises of positive law but from the simpler and more scientific teaching of philosophical doctrine. Thus the contents of the law of nature vary with the ages, but their aim is constant, it is justice; and though this species of law operates not in positive enactments, but in the minds of men, it is needless to urge that he who obtains command over minds will in the end master their institutions.

Reform and revolution cannot be produced by mere doctrines : material forces and circumstances have to be taken into account as well : moral lethargy may prove too great, the body politic too decrepit or too corrupt for sweeping changes. But the spread of doctrine claiming to pronounce judgment on positive law for the sake of justice is surely a force not to be disregarded or slighted by practical men.

It is significant that we are witnessing a revival of appeals to the law of nature in our own time. It comes from two sides. On the one hand there is a widely spreading conviction that existing systems of law are getting out of touch with fundamental requirements of modern society. It is not necessary nowadays to be a socialist in order to feel that the existing systems of positive law, which have sprung into being under the influence of feudal conceptions and of theories of free contract, will have to be largely transformed in order to meet the requirements of rising democracy. Schemes of reform and attempts at remedial legislation are being initiated everywhere; and though it would be out of the question for us to review such schemes and attempts in detail, we may notice that their growth undoubtedly testifies to a change in the leading conceptions of law.

There is another more modest contention, the admission of which, however, would undoubtedly strengthen the hands of partisans of reform. It is represented conspicuously by certain modern followers of Kant, headed by Stammler. Though granting that a law of nature as a set of perennial rules does not exist, they contend that every age ought to have its own law of nature, or rather its own " right-law " by the side of its positive law. That is, they maintain that rules of positive law have to justify their existence by reference to standards set up by the philosophical doctrine of the age. If laws are found wanting from this point of view, they ought to be corrected either by legislation or by judicial practice. Stammler's own attempt to formulate four standards by which " right-law " ought to be estimated cannot be said to be successful. It is heavily dogmatic, and leads to mere scholasticism. But the main view that in an enlightened age positive law has to be estimated by the standard of moral ideals seems to be incontestable.

I may add that in thus pleading for wider equity and greater latitude in interpreting and applying law, Stammler does not stand by any means alone. IIis view is substantiated by the spirit and acceptation of modern codes. The precise codification of laws might be expected to repress the growth of equity : but as a matter of fact, the promulgation of Codes seems to have given a new impetus to the development of a critical and reforming spirit among Continental jurists.

We tread here on ground which does not belong properly to the law of nature in the original meaning of the term. But the less ostentatious teaching as to " right-law " and " equitable " law goes much further than the discretion of judges recognized at present by English Courts would warrant. Appeals to reason and to the essence or nature of legal relations aim at systematic reforms of the law which may help to avoid social revolution.

BIBLIOGRAPHICAL NOTE

THERE is a vast literature on the subject of Jurisprudence in English as well as in foreign languages. For beginners and those interested in the general problems of law and not in its technical doctrines, the most suitable books are:

Sir William Markby, *Elements of Law* (6th edition, Oxford, 1905). The theory of Austin, which has played a very great part in the development of English Jurisprudence, is summarily stated by Professor Jethro Brown's *Austinian Theory of Law* (John Murray, 1906). Professor J. C. Gray's *Nature and Sources of Law* (Columbia University Press, 1909) approaches the subject from a different point of view, and lays special stress on the teachings of the Common Law. The theories of Continental jurists are well characterized in Korkunov's *Theory of Law* (trans. Hastings; Boston Book Co., 1909).

INDEX OF CASES

INDEX OF CASES 251

GENERAL INDEX

EUROPEAN SOCIOLOGY

An Arno Press Collection

Barth, Hans. **Wahrheit Und Ideologie.** 1945

Bayet, Albert. **Le Suicide Et La Morale.** 1922

Borkenau, Franz. **Der Übergang Vom Feudalen Zum Bürgerlichen Weltbild.** 1934

Bouglé, C[elestin]. **Bilan De La Sociologie Française Contemporaine.** 1935

Briefs, Goetz A. **The Proletariat.** 1937

Croner, Fritz. **Soziologie Der Angestellten.** 1962

Czarnowski, S[tefan]. **Le Culte Des Héros Et Ses Conditions Sociales:** Saint Patrick; Héros National De L'Irlande, 1919

Davy, Georges. **La Foi Jurée.** 1922

Ehrlich, Eugen. **Fundamental Principles Of The Sociology Of Law.** 1936

Fourastié, Jean. **The Causes Of Wealth.** 1960

Geiger, Theodor. **Aufgaben Und Stellung Der Intelligenz In Der Gesellschaft.** 1949

Geiger, Theodor. **Die Klassengesellschaft Im Schmelztiegel.** 1949

Geiger, Theodor. **Demokratie Ohne Dogma.** [1963]

Granet, Marcel. **La Pensée Chinoise.** 1934

Graunt, John. **Natural And Political Observations Mentioned In A Following Index, And Made Upon The Bills of Mortality.** 1662

Gumplowicz, Ludwig. **The Outlines of Sociology.** 1899

Guyau, M[arie Jean]. **L'Art Au Point De Vue Sociologique.** 1920

Halbwachs, Maurice. **Les Causes Du Suicide.** 1930

Halbwachs, Maurice. **Les Cadres Sociaux De La Mémoire.** 1952

Hobhouse, L[eonard] T., G[erald] C. Wheeler and M[orris] Ginsberg. **The Material Culture And Social Institutions Of The Simpler Peoples.** 1915

Hubert, René. **Les Sciences Sociales Dans L'Encyclopédie.** 1923

Jeudwine, J[ohn] W. **The Foundations Of Society And The Land.** 1925

Katz, John. **The Will To Civilization.** 1938

Lazarsfeld, Paul F. et al. **Jugend Und Beruf.** 1931

Le Bras, Gabriel. **Études De Sociologie Religieuse.** 1955/56 Two volumes in one.

Lecky, William Edward Hartpole. **History Of European Morals From Augustus To Charlemagne.** 1921. Two volumes in one.

Lederer, Emil. **Die Privatangestellten In Der Modernen Wirtschaftsentwicklung.** 1912

Le Play, F[rédérick]. **Le Réforme Sociale En France Déduite De L'Observation Comparée Des Peuples Européens.** 1864. Two volumes in one.

Levenstein, Adolf. **Die Arbeiterfrage.** 1912

Maine, Henry Sumner. **Dissertations On Early Law And Custom.** 1886

Martin Saint-Léon, Etienne. **Histoire Des Corporations De Metiers.** 1922

Michels, Roberto. **Il Proletariato E La Borghesia Nel Movimento Socialista Italiano.** 1908

Morselli, Henry. **Suicide.** 1882

Mosca, Gaetano. **Partiti E Sindacati Nella Crisi Del Regime Parlamentare.** 1949

Niceforo, Alfredo. **Kultur Und Fortschritt Im Spiegel Der Zahlen.** 1930

Palyi, Melchior, ed. **Hauptprobleme Der Soziologie.** 1923. Two volumes in one.

Picavet, F[rançois Joseph]. **Les Idéologues.** 1891

Ratzenhofer, Gustav. **Die Sociologische Erkenntnis.** 1898

Renner, Karl. **Wandlungen Der Modernen Gesellschaft.** 1953

Rigaudias-Weiss, Hilde. **Les Enquêtes Ouvrières En France Entre 1830 Et 1848.** 1936

Robson, William A. **Civilisation And The Growth Of Law.** 1935

Rowntree, B. Seebohm and May Kendall. **How The Labourer Lives.** 1913

Savigny, Frederick Charles von. **Of The Vocation Of Our Age For Legislation And Jurisprudence.** 1831

Scheler, Max, ed. **Versuche Zu Einer Soziologie Des Wissens.** 1924

Segerstedt, Torgny T. **Die Macht Des Wortes.** 1947

Siegfried, André. **Tableau Politique De La France De L'Ouest Sous La Troisieme Republique.** 1913

Sighele, Scipio. **Psychologie Des Sectes.** 1898

Sombart, Werner. **Krieg Und Kapitalismus.** 1913

Sorel, Georges. **Matériaux D'Une Théorie Du Prolétariat.** 1921

Steinmetz, S[ebald] Rudolf. **Soziologie Des Krieges.** 1929

Tingsten, Herbert. **Political Behavior.** 1937

Vierkandt, Alfred. **Gesellschaftslehre.** 1928

Vinogradoff, Paul. **Common-Sense In Law.** [1914]

von Schelting, Alexander. **Max Webers Wissenschaftslehre.** 1934